THE BIBLICAL HEBREW WORD ORDER DEBATE
A TESTING OF TWO LANGUAGE TYPOLOGIES IN THE SODOM ACCOUNT

THE BIBLICAL HEBREW WORD ORDER DEBATE
A TESTING OF TWO LANGUAGE TYPOLOGIES IN THE SODOM ACCOUNT

Jeremiah Xiufu Zuo

GlossaHouse
Wilmore, KY
www.glossahouse.com

GlossaHouse, LLC
110 Callis Circle
Wilmore, KY 40309
www.GlossaHouse.com

The Biblical Hebrew Word Order Debate:
A Testing of Two Language Typologies in the Sodom Account
Zuo, Jeremiah Xiufu
        xiv, 172 p. 22.86 cm. — (GlossaHouse thesis series; vol. 3)
        Includes bibliographical references and indices.
Library of Congress Control Number: 2017956475
ISBN-13: 978-1942697596 (Pb), 978-1942697602 (Hb)

The English and Greek fonts used to create this work are available from www.linguistsoftware.com/lgku.htm
Interior design by Fredrick J. Long
Cover design by T. Michael W. Halcomb

Dedicated to my best friend, Baz

עֶצֶם מֵעֲצָמַי וּבָשָׂר מִבְּשָׂרִי

GLOSSAHOUSE THESIS SERIES

VOLUME 3

SERIES EDITORS

T. MICHAEL W. HALCOMB
FREDRICK J. LONG
CARL S. SWEATMAN

VOLUME EDITOR

FREDRICK J. LONG

GLOSSAHOUSE THESIS SERIES

The goal of the GlossaHouse Thesis Series is to facilitate the creation and publication of innovative, affordable, and accessible scholarly resources, whether print or digital, that advance research in the areas of both ancient and modern texts and languages.

TABLE OF CONTENTS

ABBREVIATIONS

The abbreviations used throughout this book follow the standard established by the *SBL Handbook of Style*, 2nd ed. (2014). Those that do not follow the *Handbook* are listed according to abbreviation below.

AA	Adverbial Accusative
Adv	Adverb
App	Constituent in Apposition with Previous Constituent
BH	Biblical Hebrew
CNC	Compound Nominal Clause
Comp	Complement
DG	*Davidson's Hebrew Syntax*
ESV	English Standard Version
FocP	Focus Phrase
FG	Functional Grammar
GBHS	*A Guide to Biblical Hebrew Syntax*
GKC	*Gesenius' Hebrew Grammar*
HCSB	Holman Christian Standard Bible
HS	*Hebrew Studies*
HUCA	*Hebrew Union College Annual*
IBHS	*Introduction to Biblical Hebrew Syntax*
IO	Indirect Object
Inf	Infinitive
JM	Paul Joüon's *A Grammar of Biblical Hebrew*
JoTT	*Journal for Translation and Textlinguistics*
J.Pragmat	*Journal of Pragmatics*
KJV	King James Version
KUSATU	*Kleine Untersuchungen zur Sprache des Alten Testaments und seiner Umwelt*
LACUS	Linguistic Association of Canada and the United States
MNK	*A Biblical Hebrew Reference Grammar*
NASB	New American Standard Bible
Neg	Negative Particle
NIV	New International Version

NLT	New Living Translation
O	Object
P	Predicate
Part	Particle
PP	Prepositional Phrase
Pred	Predicate
Prep	Preposition
Ptcpl	Participle
Q	Interrogative Particle/Word (question)
S	Subject
SBL	Society of Biblical Literature
SBTS	Southern Baptist Theological Seminary
SIL	Summer Institute of Linguistics
SV	Subject-Verb
SVO	Subject-Verb-Object
TempP	Temporal Phrase
TopP	Topic Phrase
V	Verb
Voc	Vocative
VS	Verb-Subject
VSO	Verb-Subject-Object
WB	*Williams' Hebrew Syntax*

PREFACE

This book explores the current debate over basic word order in Biblical Hebrew. There are at least two separate but related purposes to making typological judgments about basic word order in any given language. The first is describing the language in question in the most accurate way and adding to our body of linguistic knowledge as a whole. The second involves the interpretation of speech and text in the language in question. The latter is especially pressing in light of dead languages. The obvious problem with a dead language is that living speakers cannot be consulted on what is or is not grammatical. This means that word order judgments potentially have great explanatory power. This also means that there are unique linguistic challenges to making word order judgments. I am primarily interested in how the word order judgments by Hebraists affect exegesis of the OT.

The goal I set out with is to provide a taxonomy of discourse situations and clause types wherein the different views of basic word order will produce different interpretations. Chapter 1 introduces the typological study of word order, my research question, and my methodological approach. Chapter 2 surveys the history of word order research in BH studies and English BH grammars in order to lay the groundwork for understanding the present debate. Chapter 3 introduces the linguistic discipline of discourse analysis; the concepts of pragmatics, information structure, topic, comment, and focus; and defines basic word order. Chapter 4 introduces the major voices in the word order debate. The main proposals treated are from Robert Holmstedt, Adina Moshavi, and Aaron Hornkohl. Chapter 5 is a syntactically outlined commentary on the Sodom Episode (Gen 18–19) with word order labels and commentary on marked clauses using a VSO information structure. Chapter 6 is a commentary similar to Chapter 5, but using Holmstedt's SVO information structure. Chapter 7 presents a summarizing discussion of markedness in each commentary.

I find that the readings produced by the two views largely overlap, with little exegetical consequence in a variety of discourse situations and clause types. The clauses that provide the most opportunity for significant difference of interpretation are simple *qatal* and *yiqtol* clauses (Verb-Subject or Subject-Verb) without any other fronted constituents. Of these two types, VS clauses present the most possibility for difference in interpretation. Also, clauses where the verb can be understood as irreal, but have no explicit indicators of ir-realis apart from word order, are also open to differing interpretations.

This book is a slight revision of my MA thesis completed at Trinity Evangelical Divinity School. It would not have been possible without the help and contributions of many people. I want to acknowledge all the scholars who continue to put so much work into linguistics, pragmatics, and specifically the study of Biblical Hebrew.

All of my TEDS professors deserve many thanks. They have helped me dive deeper into the disciplines of ancient Semitic languages and the world of the OT: Richard Averbeck, K. Lawson Younger, John Monson, James Hoffmeier, Dennis Magary, and Eric Tully. I especially want to thank Dr. Tully who acted as my supervisor for the thesis and Dr. Magary who acted as 2nd reader. Their suggestions and guidance, and especially their courses that sparked a desire to pursue this topic, were instrumental in completing the project. Dr. Tully's questions and Dr. Magary's eagle eye have made the work much better than it otherwise would have turned out. All remaining flaws are my own responsibility.

My education did not start at TEDS and so I want to thank all my OT professors. My college professors variously imparted a love for this portion of the canon and encouraged me to continue my studies. Thanks, Brian Peterson and Melody Deimert. My very first Biblical Hebrew teacher, Libbie Groves at Westminster Theological Seminary, deserves special mention. Those initial summer classes turned a potentially scary and daunting subject into an absolute joy for just about all who took them, whether they continued studying Biblical Hebrew or not. To this day, the way I teach Biblical Hebrew is significantly influenced by Libbie.

There are many outside of my school circles that also deserve my gratitude. I am grateful to GlossaHouse for giving me this oppor-

xiv

tunity. I have been a fan of their work ever since I received a copy of the *Illustrated Genesis*. I believe in the work they are doing and I am honored to be a part of it. Michael Halcomb and Fred Long have been incredibly patient, especially as I was delayed during my wife's recent bout with illness. They helped turn a project into a book.

I want to thank the members of Grace Covenant Church in South Elgin. Their support and prayers have meant the world to me. I am flabbergasted that so many would seek the Lord's face on my behalf during periods of sometimes overwhelming work. From the very beginning of my time at GCC, my pastor Paul Alexander has encouraged me in my studies, guided me, and helped me test my gifts and calling. The elders have shepherded me in the word of God, the deacons have served me, and the members have loved me in Christ. What more could I possibly ask for in my local body?

I have had a steadfast friend in Tom Dobrowolski. His support and friendship have been enduringly faithful over the past decade. My parents, Steven and Kathy Zuo, raised me, clothed me, and put up with me. I could not be doing what I am doing now if it were not for their support. I want to thank my children, Hadassah, Ketziah, and Mordecai for dealing with less impressive meals during crunch time when I had to spend more of my energy reading and writing instead of cooking. They have always provided me with much joy and laughter.

I continue to heap thanks on my best friend, Baz. She has truly been "bone of my bone." Without her support, love, and patience none of this could have happened. She has constantly believed in me and pushed me to get my work done, she has held me accountable, and she has been there when I needed to relax and watch a movie or play a boardgame. Thank you, Baz.

Finally, I want to thank my King and Master, Jesus the Messiah. My goal in studying has always been to be a better student and teacher of the Scriptures. I pray that, even with all of the flaws that exist in my work, God might be gloried and the church ultimately served in some small way.

Chapter 1
INTRODUCTION

The purpose of this study is to clarify how our understanding of Biblical Hebrew's basic word order contributes to the interpretation of the Bible. The motivation for this study is the desire for an ever more precise way of speaking about and teaching the language of the Hebrew Bible. Linguistic study applied to Biblical Hebrew (henceforth BH) has borne much fruit in recent years. Though this study is primarily linguistic and philological, it is my hope that its fruit would intersect with the exegetical and theological.

1.1. Linguistics and the Bible

In order to speak about language, one requires some amount of language about language. Linguistics, defined as the scientific study of language, has long had a role as an important subfield in biblical and theological studies.[1] The intersection between language study and biblical studies includes a wide variety of endeavors: theological reflection on the nature of language itself,[2] analysis and classification of language universals,[3] using language properties as a window to theological and cultural thought,[4] and the application of linguistic study to

---

[1] Walter Bodine describes linguistics as a "sister discipline" and "complement" to biblical studies. "The Study of Linguistics and Biblical Hebrew," in *Linguistics and Biblical Hebrew*, ed. Walter R. Bodine (Winona Lake, IN: Eisenbrauns, 1992), 3.

[2] Vern Poythress, *In the Beginning Was the Word: Language—A God-Centered Approach* (Wheaton, IL: Crossway, 2009).

[3] Bernard Comrie, *Language Universals and Linguistic Typology* (Chicago: University of Chicago Press, 1989).

[4] For example, chapter on "Hebrew Thought" in Jacques B. Doukhan, *Hebrew for Theologians: A Textbook for the Study of Biblical Hebrew in Relation to Hebrew Thinking* (Lanham, MD: University Press of America, 1993). Whether such work is licit is another matter. The oversimplifications of such works have been rightly criticized, e.g., by James Barr, *The Semantics of Biblical Language* (Oxford: Oxford University Press, 2000) and Moises Silva, *Biblical Words and Their Meaning: An Introduction to Lexical Semantics* (Grand Rapids: Zondervan, 1994).

the teaching and studying of the biblical languages.[5] This present study will be in the area of applied linguistics in BH.

1.2. Word Order in Linguistics

One of the recently debated issues in BH studies is the question of where BH should be placed in the schema of six possible word order language typologies. This classification question concerns the relative ordering of three main sentence constituents: subject, verb, and object.[6] Focusing on these constituents results in six possible typologies: SVO, VSO, SOV, VOS, OVS, and OSV.[7] Languages are classi-

---

[5] Peter James Silzer and Thomas John Finley provide a good example of using the fruits of linguistic study to approach teaching the biblical languages, *How Biblical Languages Work* (Grand Rapids: Kregel, 2004). For the specific application of linguistic analysis to aid in teaching particular languages see Gary A. Long, *Grammatical Concepts 101 for Biblical Hebrew* (Grand Rapids: Baker Academic, 2013), and *Grammatical Concepts 101 for Biblical Greek* (Peabody, MA: Hendrickson, 2006). For a good example of applying the fruits of linguistic study to guide interpretation and hermeneutics, see Peter Cotterell and Max Turner, *Linguistics and Biblical Interpretation* (Downers Grove, IL: InterVarsity Press, 1989).

[6] As others have has pointed out, the question is not really of "word order" but of "constituent order." Comrie, *Language Universals*, 86–87; and Aaron Hornkohl, "The Pragmatics of the X+Verb Structure in the Hebrew of Genesis: The Linguistic Functions and Associated Effects and Meanings of Intra-Clausal Fronted Constituents," *Ethnorêma* 1 (2005), 1; and Tal Goldfajin, *Word Order and Time in Biblical Hebrew Narrative* (Oxford: Oxford University Press, 1998), 9. I will employ the terminology "word order" while acknowledging that often the components in question (subject, verb, and object) are comprised of more than one word.

[7] For an introduction to the classification discussion see Matthew S. Dryer, "Order of Subject, Object, and Verb," in *The World Atlas of Language Structures*, ed. Martin Haspelmath, Matthew S. Dryer, David Gil, and Bernard Comrie (Oxford: Oxford University Press, 2005), 330–31. See also "Classifying Languages by Word Order" in Silzer and Finley, *How Biblical Languages Work*, 135–42. Silzer and Finely note the debate about the classification of Greek (138n8) but do not mention any comparable debate about BH, classifying it as VSO. This classification endeavor is credited to Joseph H. Greenberg, "Some Universals of Grammar with Particular Reference to the Order of Meaningful Elements," in *Universals of Language*, ed. Joseph H. Greenberg (Cambridge, MA: MIT Press, 1963), 73–113. It would be an oversimplification to say that every language can be neatly fit into the classical six

fied into one of these typologies based on which order is considered the normal usage of the language. Some languages have a strong tendency towards one order, with little to no possibility of variation. Others offer multiple options for the construction of any given sentence. BH is a language that has a relatively free word order.

1.3. Research Question and Intended Contribution

With the continued application of pragmatic and discourse studies to BH, a debate ensues concerning the identity of basic word order in BH. In previous scholarship, BH has usually been classified as a VSO language. Now, a growing number of scholars are arguing that BH is an SVO language. This debate has made it essential for students to be able to interact with the ramifications of the differing proposals.

It is the not the purpose of this study to examine BH in order to propose a new or complementary theory of BH word order. Instead, I have endeavored to test existing and competing views of basic word order. I pursued this project in order to understand what practical effect the differing views may have on interpretation. The specific area of interpretation that I am focusing on is the semantic and pragmatic interpretation of clauses in context. Will the different views of word order produce different interpretations of clauses in these areas? Most narrowly stated, my intent in this book is to the answer the question, "What is the practical relationship between one's view of Biblical Hebrew's basic word order and the semantic and pragmatic interpretation of clauses in classical Hebrew prose as exemplified in Gen 18–19"?

In order to answer this question, a number of subsidiary questions need to be answered. What is the history of the scholarly understanding of BH word order? What are the linguistic categories that have shaped the discussion? What are the major positions on word order in BH? Which types of clauses would be interpreted identically or near identically in the differing proposals? Which types of clauses

---

typologies or that such typological classification has always been fruitful. For a more detailed and nuanced look at word order classification see the essays in Doris L. Payne ed., *Pragmatics of Word Order Flexibility* (Amsterdam: Benjamins, 1992).

would be interpreted differently? How would these differing clause interpretations fit or not fit in their literary and discourse contexts?

The goal of answering these questions is to illuminate some of the ways in which typological word order classification judgments, when adopted by students, affect the interpretation process. I hope that this study will prove to be a suitable primer to the BH word order debate. This will require a general introduction to relevant areas of word order discussion in linguistics. Additionally, I hope to provide a clear taxonomy of the types of clauses, situations, and contexts where one must be self-consciously aware of basic word order in order to navigate and select between interpretive options.

1.4. Methodology, Limitations, and Delimitations

In order to proceed, I will begin by surveying the literature about BH word order in Chapter 2. I will first cover articles and monographs published on the topic of word order in BH. This will be followed by an examination of word order conclusions presented in introductory and reference grammars. This survey will be limited to works published in English.

In Chapter 3, I will identify the key linguistic issues that appeared in the survey of the literature and introduce them from the perspective of general linguistics. This discussion will cover discourse-analysis, pragmatics, and information structure. The concepts of topic, comment, and focus will all be defined and examined. This chapter will end with a preliminary definition of basic word order.

In Chapter 4, I will introduce and summarize the representative proposals concerning BH word order that will be tested. Much of the impetus for this debate comes from Robert Holmstedt. He has challenged the traditional VSO position in numerous publications. He devoted two chapters of his dissertation to word order, and published a number of articles defending an SVO view. For this reason, Holmstedt's work will serve as the representative of the SVO view. In light of the debate, it is ideal to have a VSO representative that has considered the newer SVO views and responded. Therefore, I sought out representatives arguing for the VSO position who have recently published significant studies. Adina Moshavi did her dissertation on word order, and published a monograph on the topic. Additionally, Aaron Hornkohl wrote his MA thesis on the topic. Moshavi limited her monograph to non-subordinate, finite clauses. Hornkohl's work provides a useful supplement to Moshavi's. Furthermore, Holmstedt, Moshavi, and Hornkohl all interact with each other in their published materials. These three have been the main voices carrying the debate in print up to this point. Therefore, they are the best choices to act as representatives: Holmstedt of SVO and Moshavi/Hornkohl of VSO.

Chapters 5 and 6 will each feature a commentary on Gen 18–19. In Chapter 5 the commentary will be from the VSO point of view as represented by Moshavi and Hornkohl. In Chapter 6, the commentary will be from the SVO point of view as represented by Holmstedt. The Hebrew text employed will be from BHS. I will not interact with text-critical issues. In the commentaries, the text will be laid out in a graphic outline. Each clause will receive a separate line. The left page side will feature linguistic notation, labeling the constituents of each clause so that their word order will be easily identifiable. I will limit commentary to only clauses that are considered marked or ambiguous.

I will summarize the data and present my conclusions in Chapter 7. I find that between the major representatives of SVO and VSO that there are few clauses that exhibit significant difference in semantic and pragmatic interpretation. Non-consecutive verb first clauses provide the most possibility for semantic variance. The VSO views allow such clauses to be interpreted as basic. The SVO position requires that the verb in such clauses to be considered fronted as a topic or focus, or indicating that the verb has an irreal force.

The central issue in this book is the interpretation of variation from basic word order. There are many types of word order variation. For the present study, I will be limiting the focus to the interpretation of fronting.[8] The literature review will reveal that fronting is one of

---

[8] A "fronted" constituent would be any word that is moved from its usual place to the front of a clause. In a VSO language, a sentence with the order of SVO

the most common types of variation and receives the most attention.

Furthermore, my study will be limited to the corpus of Gen 18–19 following the considerations outlined here. In choosing a suitable sample corpus, a number of criteria needed to be weighed. The range for BH is the Hebrew Bible. This was further limited to the early stage of BH prose, which is Genesis through 2 Kings. This limitation was done for two reasons, building on previous studies: (1) A number of those studying BH word order have limited their work to narrative on the principle that narrative is a more controlled environment to study word order consistency and variation. Only after establishing a basic word order in narrative can one move to studying word order variation in poetry; (2) even in those studies that did not limit themselves to narrative on the reasoning of (1), much work has been done in the Genesis through 2 Kings corpus, with a special emphasis on Genesis. In order to give the current studies the best possible hearing, I have sought to work in the same corpus upon which scholars have based their proposals.

Secondly, given the space limitations of a project like this, a manageable corpus needed to be defined. A chapter or two of BH is the perfect test size. This limited corpus still needed to be composed of a complete discourse, given the fact that discourse and pragmatic concerns are central to the scholarly understanding of word order variation. In order to illustrate fine differences and make the most fruitful comparisons of competing proposals, it is necessary to test them over an entire discourse.

Thirdly, it is desired to have an equal amount of both third person narration and direct speech. It is obvious from previous statistical studies that direct speech evidences more word order variation than narration. There is also significant debate over which type of discourse is better ground for establishing basic word order.[9] I sought a

---

would be said to have the subject fronted.

[9] Robert Longacre argues for narrative while Pamela Downing argues for direct speech. See Longacre, "Left Shifts in Strongly VSO Languages," in *Word Order in Discourse*, ed. Pamela Downing and Michael Noonan (Amsterdam: Benja-

good mix because this study cannot give space to deciding between these positions.

Finally, the study requires a corpus with as many non-consecutive or *qatal* and *yiqtol* forms as possible.[10] Regardless of how scholars incorporate the data from *weqatal* and *wayyiqtol* forms into their basic word order conclusions, these forms are fixed as clause initial. Any clauses that contain a consecutive form must be VS if an explicit subject is included. In order to encounter and examine word order variation, our corpus needs to have large amounts of the non-consecutive *qatal* and *yiqtol* forms.

The selection process for the sample corpus worked by applying the given criteria in reverse. I created a search with Accordance Bible Software for chapters of the Bible with either *qatal* or *yiqtol* forms. I vetted the chapters with the highest amounts by the other criteria. The single chapter from the classical corpus with the most *qatal* and *yiqtol* forms is 1 Kings 8 (109 forms). However, this chapter is dominated by direct speech and cannot be viewed as a distinct discourse unit. Upon further inspection, Gen 18–19 also contained a combined total of 109 *qatal* or *yiqtol* forms, but further met the other criteria: it has a good mix of direct speech and narrative and it covers the entire Sodom episode.[11]

---

mins, 1995), 331–54; and Downing, "Word Order in Discourse: By Way of Introduction," in *Word Order in Discourse*, ed. Pamela Downing and Michael Noonan (Amsterdam: Benjamins, 1995), 1–28.

[10] A word about terminology is in order. I have opted to use the morphological designations (*qatal*/*yiqtol*/*weqatal*/*wayyiqtol*) when referring to the forms in the BH verbal system. This avoids many of the errant and confusing ideas bound up with older terminology based on "converting/consecutive" waws. This is still not perfect, but the morphological designations suit the purposes of this book well enough. For a good summary of the issues and a more fruitful way forward, see John A. Cook, "Reconsidering the So-called Vav-Consecutive," (paper presented at the Annual Meeting of the SBL, New Orleans, LA, 23 November 2009).

[11] For a thorough literary defense of Gen 18–19 as a self-contained unit, see David W. Cotter, *Genesis in Berit Olam: Studies in Hebrew Narrative & Poetry* (Collegeville, MN: Liturgical Press, 2003), 113–16.

Chapter 2
WORD ORDER IN PAST RESEARCH
AND ENGLISH BIBLICAL HEBREW GRAMMARS

This chapter will survey word order studies in the BH literature. It will also cover the major English grammars in detail. The consensus has been to see BH being a VSO language. I will focus on studies as they relate to this consensus, present it, or depart from it. This will help one understand the issues and positions that preceded the current VSO vs. SVO debate.

2.1. Summary of Older Research on Word Order in BH
The history of word order studies in BH has shown a decided and traceable development. Older and vague frameworks gave way to new and more precise descriptions. The newer frameworks have been based on modern uses of discourse and pragmatic categories. I will trace this development chronologically, acknowledging that space precludes an exhaustive treatment.[1]

Modern scholars studying word order have tended to divide BH by clause type, speaking of nominal and verbal clauses.[2] Most scholars hold that each clause type has a different basic word order. One of the most influential studies on BH word order has been the

---

[1] Adina Moshavi, *Word Order in the Biblical Hebrew Finite Clause* (Winona Lake, IN: Eisenbrauns, 2010), 18–47; She provides a summary specifically on the research of the functions of fronting. She helpfully categorizes studies into three types of solutions offered: the emphasis model, the foreground-background model, and the information-structure model.

[2] While I will refer to nominal clauses generally in the following, it is outside the scope of this work to examine the discourse function of nominal clauses in detail. For a good introduction to that issue see, Lenart J. de Regt, "Macrosyntactic Functions of Nominal Clauses Referring to Participants," in *The Verbless Clause in Biblical Hebrew: Linguistic Approaches,* ed. Cynthia L. Miller (Winona Lake, IN: Eisenbrauns, 1999), 286–96.

work of Francis I. Andersen on the nominal clause.[3] Andersen criticizes earlier studies that treat Subject-Predicate (S-P) as the basic order and ascribe deviances to "emphasis." His initial complaint mirrors one of the impetuses for this book, "Explanations of exceptions [of normal word order] are often given in terms of concepts like *emphasis* or *importance*, which have no empirical status."[4] Andersen went on to identify different types of clauses that each conveyed different semantic information. According to Andersen, basic word order would be different depending on the semantic purpose of the clause.

Andersen summarized his conclusions into nine rules governing the grammar of nominal clauses.[5] In Andersen's model, he also correlates word order and semantics with syntactic observations. Clauses that have definite subjects and definite predicates also have total semantic overlap between the subject and predicate. These are called clauses of identification and have the order S-P. Clauses that have a definite subject and an indefinite predicate have only partial semantic overlap. These clauses indicate a class to which the subject belongs. These are called clauses of classification and have the order P-S. Clauses with participles as the predicate are considered in a different category.[6] Declarative statements with participles have a normal S-P order, while precative statements have a normal P-S order.

Andersen also connected word order to circumstantiality. Circumstantial clauses have S-P order and usually begin with a conjunction. Clauses that began with the conjunction and are of classifying nature still exhibit S-P order. The correspondence between circumstantiality and S-P order is so consistent that Andersen argues that circumstantiality can be identified by word order alone, apart from the

---

[3] His work is limited to the Pentateuch but involves a study of every verbless clause in that corpus. Francis I. Andersen, *The Hebrew Verbless Clause in the Pentateuch* (Nashville: Abingdon, 1970).

[4] Andersen, *Hebrew Verbless Clause,* 18.

[5] Ibid., 39–50.

[6] Andersen considered clauses with a participle as the predicate to be verbal and distinct from classifying clauses (*Hebrew Verbless Clause,* 34).

presence of the conjunction. Older descriptions connected circumstantiality to the use of the disjunctive waw.

Though Andersen has been widely adopted, there have been
criticisms and refinements.[7] In the wake of the pragmatic discussion,
many have returned to seeing S-P as the basic word order for nominal
clauses. However, this has not been a backwards movement so much
as a course correction. Andersen describes ideas such as the psychological subject as "exegetical inferences and not grammatical categories."[8] The recent work of discourse grammar has sought to establish
the psychological subject (i.e., topic) and other such ideas as grammatical categories.[9] One of the turning point studies is Muraoka's
Emphatic Words and Structures in Biblical Hebrew.[10] His opening
comments have become a watchword in BH word order studies;

> A perusal of the literature relative to our subject has made it
> quite clear that the term 'emphasis' is often too rashly called in,
> like a pinch-hitter in the baseball game, without much thought
> being given to precisely what is meant by the term nor, more
> importantly, to the question why the writer or speaker possibly
> felt the need for an emphatic form or construction. The impres-
> sion is thus created that 'emphasis' is a ready panacea for He-
> braists' (and Semitists') headaches of all sorts.[11]

---

[7] Jacob Hoftijzer, "The Hebrew Verbless Clause in the Pentateuch," *VT* 23
(1973): 446–510; Randall Buth, "Word Order in the Verbless Clause: A Generative-Functional Approach," in *The Verbless Clause in Biblical Hebrew: Linguistic
Approaches*, ed. Cynthia L. Miller (Winona Lake, IN: Eisenbrauns, 1999), 94–100;
and Takamitsu Muraoka, *Emphatic Words and Structures in Biblical Hebrew* (Leiden: Brill, 1985), 6.

[8] Andersen, *Hebrew Verbless Clause*, 17.

[9] For example, Buth's proposal in "Word Order in the Verbless Clause,"
100–106.

[10] This is a revised version of Muraoka's earlier dissertation, "Emphasis in
Biblical Hebrew" (PhD Diss., Hebrew University in Jerusalem, 1969).

[11] Muraoka, *Emphatic Words*, xi.

We can detect the principle insight of Muraoka's work in this initial quote. The important issue is the question of why an emphatic word order might be used. Muraoka did not abandon emphasis as a term or explanation, but noted that emphasis was not a deep enough answer to the question "why this form/structure"? Emphasis may be what a particular word order accomplishes, but then one must know, why emphasize this or that word? When scholars start asking this question, more fruitful discussions of word order, moving beyond the isolated sentence, begin to materialize.

Muraoka states that "normal/relative" order of verbal clauses is V-S. He means the statistically dominant order, excepting *wayyiqtol* clauses from the count.[12] From the position of statistical dominance, Muraoka seeks to understand deviations from the normal order. Another of his key working points is the idea that emphasis is not always intended on the fronted subject. He notes that emphasis is a relevant factor in many instances, but cannot account for all S-V clauses. Muraoka provides a taxonomy of S-V clauses that reappears in his revision of Paul Joüon's grammar.

Barry L. Bandstra is one of the first to provide clear descriptions of the functions of emphasis in modern linguistic terminology and categories. In his 1986 paper, presented in the Linguistics and Biblical Hebrew section of the SBL Annual Meeting, Bandstra introduces the concept of given and new information to BH studies.[13] He

---

[12] Muraoka, "[W]e are not interested in discussing the theory that [VS] order is normal because action is the most important piece of information to be conveyed by this sentence type called verbal clause. In other words, by saying that V-S is the normal word order we do not mean that it is logically or intrinsically so, but simply statistically" (*Emphatic Words*, 30). Muraoka agrees with others who argue that the clauses containing the *wayyiqtol* or *weqatal* should be excluded given the absence of the possibility of a S-V order. His statistical assessment is apart from *wayyiqtol* and *weqatal* clauses.

[13] Published later as Barry L. Bandstra, "Word Order and Emphasis in Biblical Hebrew Narrative: Syntactic Observations on Genesis 22 from a Discourse Perspective," in *Linguistics and Biblical Hebrew*, ed. Walter R. Bodine (Winona Lake, IN: Eisenbrauns, 1992), 109–23.

argues that it is intuitively known and demonstrable that the information structure of language is generally given-new—i.e., given information tends to come before new information in a clause.[14] Bandstra assumes that in BH, VSO is the "expected" and "most frequent"
order of constituents in narrative verbal clauses.[15] After examining
various word orders that occur in BH, Bandstra concludes by giving a
more precise definition of emphasis—"Emphasis can now be more
profitably understood as the discourse effect of placing new information in the position where given information is typically found."[16]
Therefore, the first position of a clause is not inherently emphatic. The
movement of types of information is the most relevant for determining
emphasis. Bandstra concludes that topicalization is a better term for
what was previously called emphasis by fronting.[17]

Karel Jongeling presents one of the earlier attempts to defend
VSO as the basic order using modern linguistic approaches. He gives a
detailed count of the various verb clauses in the book of Ruth. By his
count, only 20% of the clauses with an explicit subject are S-V. This is
enough for Jongeling to conclude that VSO is "best considered to be
the basic order of classical Hebrew."[18] However, it is clear that what

---

[14] Bandstra, "Word Order and Emphasis," 114.

[15] Ibid., 115. However, this does not mean that the verbal constituent is
given information as Bandstra himself recognizes. Rather, "given and new are based
on discourse and cannot be determined for any clause as it stands isolated from text
and context." Therefore, the given-new order is a relative order. This means that
apart from the fixed rule of Hebrew being a verb first language, the regular positions
of information is determined by their informational status.

[16] Ibid., 120.

[17] Although it is outside the scope of this work, Bandstra covers examples of
post-verbal fronting as well. His system can be summarized: when a constituent is
moved to another constituent's normal position it is given prominence by virtue of
the disconnect between its informational status and new position. A new object
where we would expect given information is jarring. In VOS orders, the object has
been fronted above the subject and has become the topic of the clause.

[18] Karel Jongeling, "On the VSO Character of Hebrew," in *Studies in Hebrew and Aramaic Syntax: Presented to Professor J. Hoftijzer on the Occasion of
His Sixty-Fifth Birthday*, ed. K. Jongeling, H. L. Murre-van den Berg and L. Van

Jongeling means in this sentence by "basic" is statistically dominant. Jongeling goes on to argue that VSO is also the "standard" order, or the starting-point from which other orders are derived. He states, based on the criteria of economy, VSO should be taken as standard. This is because it is easier to describe SVO clauses as variations of VSO clauses rather than vice versa.

Jongeling's main argument is a typological comparison with Welsh, a VSO language. The gist of this type of argument is to identify features of one language whose basic word order is given and compare those with the features of the language in question.[19] BH shares arrangement features with Welsh that are said to be typological of VSO languages. These features can be summarized as displaying the natural order of modified-modifier. Jongeling also notes other correspondences; such as the use of a resumptive pronoun, compound nominal sentences, the existence of pronominal suffixes, and reinforcement of the pronominal suffix with an independent pronoun form. He notes that scholars have not determined whether these latter features correspond to the VSO nature of the languages.[20]

Randall Buth has published numerous studies on word order.[21] Buth has followed and utilized Simon Dik's functional grammar (FG).[22] Dik postulated a "pragmatic position" at the beginning of the

---

Rompey (Leiden: Brill, 1991), 106.

[19] Such an argument is based on the initial work of Joseph Greenberg in identifying ostensible typological universals; Joseph H. Greenberg, *Language Universals with Special Reference to Feature Hierarchies* (The Hague: Mouton, 1966).

[20] Jongeling, "On the VSO Character," 107–9.

[21] See Buth, "Word Order in the Verbless Clause"; "Functional Grammar, Hebrew and Aramaic: An Integrated, Textlinguistic Approach to Syntax," in *Discourse Analysis of Biblical Literature: What It Is and What It Offers*, ed. Walter R. Bodine (Atlanta: SBL Press, 1995), 77–102; "Topic and Focus in Hebrew Poetry: Psalm 51," in *Language in Context: Essays for Robert E. Longacre*, ed. S. J. J. Hwang and W. Merrifield (Dallas: SIL Internationl, 1995), 83–96; and "Word Order in Aramaic from the Perspective of Functional Grammar and Discourse Analysis," (Ph.D. thesis, University of California, 1987).

[22] See Simon Dik, *Functional Grammar* (Dordrecht: Foris, 1981); and *The Theory of Functional Grammar: Part I: The Structure of the Clause* (Dordrecht:

clause in every language. A constituent can fill this position in order to mark it with a pragmatic function. The word order of English would be PPosition-Subject-Verb-Object. Because of the existence of the "p-position" as part of the basic word order, one can place constituents other than the subject and verb in it without affecting the normal word order. From this point of view, the basic word order is expected to follow any fronted constituents. The fact that Hebrew has an abundance of XVS clauses compared to very few XSV clauses (where X represents any constituent other than the subject and verb) is evidence that BH is VS language and consequently all SV orders are marked.[23]

Buth also attempts to provide a unified theory of describing marking functions. He accounts for the notions of foreground/background, topic, and focus together. Buth changes the usual 'topic' to 'contextualizing constituent' (CC). The CC is defined as a marked constituent that signals the reader how they are to relate the clause to the surrounding context.[24] Focus is the most important information to be conveyed by the clause. In this understanding, CC and focus are as different as "day from night."[25] Focus is the important information; the CC tells the listener how to add that information to their mental world. Buth unifies topic and focus with foreground and background by positing a fusion of functions so that the CC can be

---

Foris Publications, 1989). Other studies based on FG include Michael Rosenbaum, *Word-Order Variation in Isaiah 40–55* (Assen: Van Gorcum, 1997); Rosenbaum works from an assumed basic VSO order, and posits three initial positions (P2,, Pdp, and P1) and one post position (P3) in keeping with Dik. The shape of the clause is P2,-Pdp-P1-V-S-O-P3. Any constituent can be "moved." Rosenbaum follows Dik in that, strictly speaking, constituents are placed into one of the positions in order to mark it for a pragmatic function and not moved from a prior position. Rosenbaum's pragmatic functions include topic, theme, setting, focus, tail, vocative, and parenthetical information. See Dik, *Theory of Functional Grammar*, 334.

[23] Buth, "Word Order in the Verbless Clause," 79–81.
[24] Buth, "Functional Grammar," 84.
[25] Ibid.

used for not only the topic, but also the setting, paragraph/unit board-ers, and dramatic pause.[26]

Studies continue to refine and apply these linguistic advances.[27] BH linguists currently wrestle with proposed theoretical grammars and incorporating data from cognate studies. There is still much work to be done. Newer studies have also begun the difficult work of examining the intersection of word order phenomena and poetics.[28]

2.2. Word Order in Introductory Grammars

My study has found Katsuomi Shimasaki's observation to be true: "The word order of biblical Hebrew does not seem to have been one of the central issues of grammarians in the past. Introductory grammar books hardly mention it, or, if they do, the treatment is only cursory."[29] In order to understand the frameworks that underlie the modern debate, the following sections will survey BH grammars. I have attempted to survey the major English grammars. Not every

---

[26] Ibid., 89.

[27] Jean-Marc Heimerdinger, *Topic, Focus and Foreground in Ancient Hebrew Narratives* (Sheffield: Sheffield Academic, 1999); "An Overview of Hebrew Narrative Syntax," in *Narrative Syntax and the Hebrew Bible: Papers of the Tilburg Conference 1996*, ed. E. J. van Wolde (Leiden: Brill, 1997), 1–20; "Explaining Fronting in Biblical Hebrew," *JNSL* 25.2 (1999): 173–86; "The Function of Word Order in Old Hebrew—with Special Reference to Cases where a Syntagmeme Precedes a Verb in Joshua," *JNSL* 17 (1991): 129–44; "Towards a Better Understanding of Biblical Hebrew Word Order (Review of Walter Gross's *Die Satzteilfolge im Verbal-satz alttestamentlicher Prosa*)," *JNSL* 25.1 (1999): 277–300; and van der Merwe, Christo H.J., and Eep Talstra, "Biblical Hebrew Word Order: The Interface of Information Structure and Formal Features," *ZAH* 15/16 (2002/2003): 68–107; Much of the fruit of van der Merwe's studies have been summarized in my treatment of the grammar which he co-wrote.

[28] Nicholas P. Lunn, *Word-Order Variation in Biblical Hebrew Poetry: Differentiating Pragmatics and Poetics* (Exeter: Paternoster, 2006); Sherry Lynn Fariss, "Word Order in Biblical Hebrew Poetry" (PhD thesis, The University of Texas, 2003); Sebastian Floor, "Poetic Fronting in a Wisdom Poetry Text: The Information Structure of Proverbs 7," *JNSL* 31.1 (2005): 23–58.

[29] Katsuomi Shimasaki, *Focus Structure in Biblical Hebrew* (Bethesda, MD: CDL, 2002), v.

grammar had much if anything to say about word order. Those that do are treated here in chronological order.

The idiosyncratic terminology used by each grammar for basic word order (e.g., typical, normal, usual, etc.) is preserved in each discussion below in order to highlight how each grammar has spoken of basic word order. Such words are not always simple synonyms and the author's choice can be a subtle indication of an essential conceptual framework behind their view of word order. The presentation of each grammar as a whole may depart from the vocabulary of any given author in order to rephrase the essential content in light of the terminology employed in this book. Especially idiosyncratic terminology from each grammar is defined.

2.2.1. Weingreen (1959)

A Practical Grammar for Classical Hebrew has been a standard classroom grammar for almost eighty years. However, it says almost nothing about basic word order. The only brief comment in the 2nd edition is in a small-print note describing the suffixed formation of *qatal* verbs (Section 29. Note d).[30] Weingreen observes that "[i]t appears that in Hebrew thought the general or main idea is first expressed and is limited in its application by a following word or particle." He cites the *qatal* ("perfect conjugation" in Weingreen) as an example of this phenomenon: the main idea (the verbal root) is followed a pronominal particle that limits the application. Weingreen extends this observation by listing further examples of similar structuring in BH— possession ("my man" = אישי), attributive adjective ("a good man" = איש טוב) and a simple sentence "the man said" = אמר האיש.

For Weingreen, word order is determined by a notion of the primacy of an idea to the meaning of any given unit. Main ideas come first. Those things that would be considered modifiers come second. The verbal action comes first, followed by the subject which specifies who does the action.

---

[30] J. Weingreen, *A Practical Grammar for Classical Hebrew* (Oxford: Oxford University Press, 1959), 57.

2.2.2. Lambdin (1971)

An Introduction to Biblical Hebrew discusses word order in two different sections. In Section 45, Lambdin notes that the usual word order is VSOA (where "A" stands for any adverbial elements). After giving some examples, he notes that "[i]t is by no means unusual to find the subject or some other element before the verb..."[31] The reasons given for these deviations are "emphasis" or a change conditioned by an "interclause relationship."

Lambdin returns to elaborate on the aforementioned interclause relationships in Section 132.[32] The most relevant portions of his discussion concern the nature of disjunctive clauses. Lambdin states that clauses joined by a waw conjunction are either conjunctive-sequential or disjunctive. Disjunctive clauses are defined as those in which the marked clause is not sequential with the previous clause. Sequentiality is defined as following temporally or logically from the previous clause. Lambdin notes that disjunctive clauses are primarily signaled by a non-verb following the conjunction. Hence, the term disjunctive waw. The normal VS order can be shifted to XV in order to mark a disjunctive clause. This means that all clauses that do not use a finite verbal form and all negative clauses must be disjunctive. They cannot follow temporally or logically from the previous clause.

2.2.3. Kelly/Burden/Crawford (1994)

Biblical Hebrew: An Introductory Grammar gives a succinct and simple description of BH word order. The normal order of the verbal sentence is VSO. Variations on this word order are used to emphasize whichever part of speech is placed first.[33] This is the traditional position stated but not elaborated on.

---

[31] Thomas O. Lambdin, *An Introduction to Biblical Hebrew* (New York: Schribner's Sons, 1971), 39.

[32] Ibid., 162–63.

[33] Paige H. Kelly, Terry L. Burden, and Timothy G. Crawford, *A Handbook to Biblical Hebrew: An Introductory Grammar* (Grand Rapids: Eerdmans, 1994), 87.

2.2.4. Seow (1995)

A *Grammar for Biblical Hebrew* presents a BH word order that accounts for more than just the standard three sentence constituents. According to Seow, the "normal" word order in Hebrew prose is CVSIO.[34] "C" represents circumstance and this slot can be filled by any adverb or adverbial phrase (or even particles). "I" represents the indirect object (i.e., objects of the prepositions לְ or אֶל). He gives two examples of his normal word order.[35]

(1) אָז שָׁמַע הַמֶּלֶךְ אֲלֵיהֶם

2 Chron 24:17 (CVSI)

(2) נָתַן יְהוָה לָכֶם אֶת־הָאָרֶץ

Josh 2:9 (VSIO)

Seow notes that the word order is not rigidly fixed. He gives four reasons for what he calls "disrupted word order." These reasons are the introduction of a new subject, the inclusion of a redundant independent personal pronoun (particularly in parenthetical comments), emphasis, and contrast. Seow also mentions in an excursus on Hebrew poetry, "poetic texts may take license for stylistic reasons."[36] This is described as "variable" word order and no further account of poetic word order is provided.

In Seow there is the most full explanation of the classical position. The basic word order is VSO (with the possibility of further specification concerning other constituents). This order is deviated from for particular pragmatic reasons in prose. It is also deviated from for stylistic reasons in poetry.

2.2.5. Bornemann (1998)

A *Grammar of Biblical Hebrew* gives a unique description of BH word order. Sentences are divided into the usual two types: nomi-

---

[34] C. L. Seow, *A Grammar for Biblical Hebrew* (Nashville: Abingdon Press, 1995), 149–50.

[35] Ibid., 150.

[36] Ibid., 158–59.

nal and verbal. However, the normal word order of all sentences is described as subject-predicate. Subjects that follow verbs are said to be "extensions of the subject already expressed in the verb." Such VS word order would not violate the Subject-Predicate word order. On this basis, Bornemann criticizes the characterization of normal word order in BH as Verb-Subject and calls such a conclusion inaccurate.[37]

Bornemann's treatment also approaches the idea of a "free word order."[38] Though subject-predicate is said to be the normal word order, Bornemann also maintains that it is "better to say that the order of words in a sentence ... is determined by what the author is doing."[39] Various functions might require different word orders. Bornemann reiterates later "the actual word order of any sentence is determined by the writer's style and emphases."[40] No particular functions are associated with any particular word order, making the section difficult to apply. The general impression is clear enough: BH word order is free and varies according to authorial intent. Though Bornemann does not use this verbiage, his work makes it plain that he considers word order dependent on function in the discourse.

2.2.6. Ross (2001)

Introducing Biblical Hebrew briefly treats word order in two sections in Lesson 54.[41] Nominal and verbal sentences are dealt with separately. The first section treats word order in nominal sentences. The second treats word order in verbal sentences.

Ross is in the minority in not following Andersen on nominal clauses.[42] Ross describes the word order of such clauses as sub-

---

[37] Robert Bornemann, *A Grammar of Biblical Hebrew* (Eugene, OR: Wipf & Stock, 2011), 217–18.

[38] Languages that are said to have no basic word order are described as "free order languages."

[39] Bornemann, *Grammar of Biblical Hebrew*, 218.

[40] Ibid., 222.

[41] Allen P. Ross, *Introducing Biblical Hebrew* (Grand Rapids: Baker Academic, 2001), 416–24.

[42] Ibid., 416–17.

ject-predicate because the subject is "prominent." Ross lists three exceptions to this word order due to "fixed grammatical and stylistic orders." (1) Simple predicate adjectives come first in a nominal sentence. Though if the subject is complex (i.e., "men of Sodom") it has prominence and comes first, (2) in interrogative sentences the predicate comes first, and (3) in dependent clauses the predicate comes first.

Word order in verbal sentences is described as verb first.[43] When another element of the sentence is fronted before the verb, it is said to be given "prominence." Though not described in any detail, it seems Ross' use of prominence is equivalent to "emphasis" used by other authors. Ross ends by cautioning that there may be other reasons for variation in normal word order (he points to poetic parallelism and balance as examples).

2.2.7. Walker-Jones (2003)

Hebrew for Biblical Interpretation says little about word order. Walker-Jones notes that when an explicit subject is expressed it "normally follows the verb rather than precedes it..."[44] Walker-Jones does discuss the disjunctive and parenthetical waws. These two are treated together as simply the disjunctive waw by most of the other grammars. Walker-Jones describes them as waws that are prefixed to anything other than finite verb and serve to interrupt the narrative. Disjunctive waws can introduce contrast or start a new episode. Parenthetical waws can provide circumstantial or explanatory (epexegetical) information.

2.2.8. Futato (2003)

Beginning Biblical Hebrew provides only two sentences on word order (7.7 and 7.8).[45] The typical word order is VSO. When ei-

---

[43] Ibid., 417.

[44] Arthur W. Walker-Jones, *Hebrew for Biblical Interpretation* (Atlanta: SBL Press, 2003), 51.

[45] Mark D. Futato, *Beginning Biblical Hebrew* (Winona Lake, IN: Eisenbrauns, 2003), 40–41.

ther the subject or object is fronted before the verb, it is receiving emphasis. Futato gives two examples of emphasis: in both examples the
item emphasized is being contrasted with another possible item.

2.2.9. Kittel/Hoffer/Wright (2004)

Biblical Hebrew: A Text and Workbook is a completely induc-
tive grammar. BH is taught by walking through actual verses and sentences. It only briefly mentions that BH is normally VS.[46] No discussion of deviation from this word order is given.

2.2.10. Fuller/Choi (2006)

An Invitation to Biblical Hebrew has a greater focus on phonology than all the other grammars surveyed. The self-consciously
deductive approach adopted by the authors emphasizes phonology first
and then morphology. Little space is provided for issues of syntax. BH
is briefly described as a VSO language. Subjects before the verb are
placed there for emphasis.[47]

2.2.11. Pratico/Van Pelt (2007)

Word order is treated in Chapter 23 of *Basics of Biblical Hebrew*. Pratico and Van Pelt describe the normal word order of BH as
VSO. Numerous exceptions to this word order are listed in 23.3: e.g.,
the verb being preceded by adverbs, הנה, negatives, personal pronoun
for emphasis, etc. However, no distinction is made between what is a
true exception to VSO word order and what is the normal placement of
additional sentence constituents. Pratico and Van Pelt summarize
"...the presence of any of the sentence components listed above does
not necessarily alter the verb-subject-object sentence arrangement."[48]

---

[46] Victoria Hoffer, Bonnie Pedrotti Kittel, and Rebecca Abts Wright, *Biblical Hebrew: Text and Workbook* (New Haven: Yale University Press, 2004), 8.

[47] Russell T. Fuller and Kyoungwon Choi, *Invitation to Biblical Hebrew: A
Beginning Grammar* (Grand Rapids: Kregel, 2006), 26.

[48] Gary D. Pratico and Miles V. Van Pelt, *Basics of Biblical Hebrew
Grammar* (Grand Rapids: Zondervan, 2014), 272.

In sections on the syntax of the subject and object respectively, Practico/Van Pelt notes that either can precede the verb for emphasis and that "there are other reasons for this type of variation."[49]

The most significant portion of their presentation is found in section 23.8: Disjunctive Waw. The disjunctive waw is described as being prefixed to non-verbal forms. It functions to interrupt the narrative. Although the disjunctive waw is not explicitly called an exception to normal VSO word order by Pratico and Van Pelt, that is what its use requires. Four functions of the waw+SV word order are provided.[50] These are described as the major but not the only possible functions: parenthetical (clause provides helpful explanatory information), circumstantial (clause provides circumstances that are useful/necessary for understanding the main action of the narrative), contrastive (clause introduces an idea that contrasts with a previous idea), and introductory (clause begins a new narrative or major section within a narrative). Admittedly, the distinction between parenthetical and circumstantial is hard to conceptualize absent definitions that are more precise. Pratico and Van Pelt themselves admit that the distinction "can be subtle."[51]

2.2.12. Garret/DeRouchie (2009)

A Modern Grammar for Biblical Hebrew does not contain a particular section or specific discussion of word order. Word order does occasionally appear in discussions throughout the grammar. Particularly, verb-first word order is used as a guide for distinguishing between irreal and real *yiqtols*. Irreal *yiqtols* are said to employ a VS word order.[52]

2.2.13. Webster (2009)

The Cambridge Introduction to Biblical Hebrew describes

---

[49] Ibid., 276–77.

[50] Ibid., 278–81.

[51] Ibid., 281.

[52] Duane A. Garret and Jason S. DeRouchie, *A Modern Grammar for Biblical Hebrew* (Nashville: B&H Academic, 2009), 220.

word order from a discourse oriented approach. Word order in Web-ster's grammar is related to each clause's function in the narrative. Verb first is described as the basic order in narrative. This is because the "backbone" of BH narrative is the preterite/*wayyiqtol*. Webster explains verb first word order as the result of the preterite being a "frozen form combining the conjunction with this otherwise archaic verb form."[53] A verb first word order is not necessarily intrinsic to BH as a language in this case. Clauses which begin with an element other than the verb are described (in narrative) as "interruptions in verb sequences" and "marked or distinguished by their word order."[54] These clauses are set in contrast to the preterite that carries the main storyline. Webster cautions that there are many possible functions of such interruptions but does not go into detail.

> [Interruptions] often do more than mark emphasis on a distinct subject. They may mark a break in the scenes of the story...They can set the stage for the story or section of the story to begin, describe the circumstances of another action, introduce new characters, present contrasting information, or perform other functions.[55]

2.2.14. Holmstedt/Cook (2013)

Beginning Biblical Hebrew: A Grammar and Illustrated Reader incorporates word order interpretation at various points. Holmstedt and Cook hold that BH is a Subject-Verb language like English.[56] The reversed order, Verb-Subject, is described as "predictably common" and is said, often to be the result of a linguistic phenomenon known as *triggered inversion*—word order variation that occurs in certain syntactic environments. VS word ordered is triggered in BH whenever any

---

[53] Brian L. Webster, *The Cambridge Introduction to Biblical Hebrew* (Cambridge: Cambridge University Press, 2009), 263.

[54] Ibid., 263–65.

[55] Ibid., 267.

[56] John A. Cook and Robert D. Holmstedt, *Beginning Biblical Hebrew: A Grammar and Illustrated Reader* (Grand Rapids: Baker Academic, 2013), 60.

other sentence element comes before the subject and the verb. These other elements can be grammatical words such as כִּי, relatives, negatives אַז, פֶּן, etc., as well as full phrases or focus words. When a word or phrase is first, whether obligatorily or fronted for some particular reason, it will trigger VS word order. Some particles such as the waw conjunction and עַתָּה do not generally trigger word order inversion. Holmstedt and Cook also note that such inversion does not occur in nominal clauses, including clauses with participles as the predicate.

Basic order can be changed by a desire to mark focus or topic. In such a case, an element would be fronted in order to indicate its status as either the focus or topic. The subject or the verb can be focused. Even in cases when neither the subject nor verb is marked for focus or topic, if another element is fronted as a topic or focus it will trigger inversion to VS word order.

Word order is also used as a diagnostic feature in distinguishing between moods.[57] The basic word order of SV conveys real (indicative) mood and inverted word order (not the result of triggered inversion) conveys irreal mood. Irreal clauses can front their subjects for focus, and in such cases, they invert back to subject-verb word order. In such cases, the irreal mood is recognized by context, form, or modal particles and the word order is used to focus the subject.[58]

2.2.15. Summary

Almost all of the introductory grammars have at least something to say about word order. There is, unfortunately, a muddle of different terminologies. When the grammars are surveyed and synthesized, it becomes apparent that there is much unity in what is being said. If it were not for the presence of Holmstedt/Cook and Bornemann in this survey, the introductory grammars would not indicate that there is any major debate over BH's basic word order. The only debate that would remain would be over the functions of word orders that deviate from the basic order. Below are six summarizing observations:

---

[57] Ibid., 66–67.
[58] Ibid., 114–15.

1. Some grammars give a psychological explanation for word order: the idea that what is most prominent or important comes first in a clause (Weingreen, Ross).
2. Most grammars that take a position on basic word order hold that BH is VSO or simply VS (Bornemann and Holmstedt/Cook being the notable exceptions).
3. Most grammars explain all or at least some instances of SV word order as being for "emphasis" on the subject (Futato, Ross, Seow).
4. Some grammars are more explicit and define "emphasis" further with concepts like "contrast" (Futato, Seow).
5. Some grammars highlight a discourse function for word order: i.e., word orders signal the relationships that sentences have with the larger paragraph or narrative (Lambdin, Webster, Seow, Pratico/Van Pelt, Bornemann).
6. Some grammars note the relationship between word order and certain semantic values, such as mood (Garret/DeRouchie, Holmstedt/Cook).[59]

2.3. Word Order in Reference Grammars

The reference grammars of BH treat word order in a more detailed fashion than the introductory grammars surveyed. The presentations range. Some display greater synthesis, such as found in Merwe/Naudé/Kroeze. Others, like Williams/Beckman, list and comment on various word orders without any attempt to synthesize these into a unified framework.

2.3.1. Gesenius/Kautzsch/Cowley (1922)

Gesenius' Hebrew Grammar has been a standard, having 28 editions in the original German. The 2nd English edition by A.E.

---

[59] This builds on the work of E. J. Revell and Vincent DeCaen. See Revell, "The System of the Verb in Standard Biblical Prose," *HUCA* 60 (1989): 1–37; and DeCaen, "On the Placement and Interpretation of the Verb in Standard Biblical Hebrew Prose," (PhD thesis, University of Toronto, 1995).

Cowley remains a fixture in English Hebrew studies.[60] GKC divides its treatment of word order between nominal and verbal clauses. Earlier editions of the grammar followed the Arabic grammarians in defining a nominal clause as any clause that started with a noun. GKC now follows the more usual linguistic definition of a nominal clause: any clause that does not have a finite verb as the predicate. However, GKC does call the Arabic view "relatively correct" (140.f) as far as it makes a distinction between clauses that begin with a verb and clauses that begin with a noun.[61]

Semantically speaking, nominal clauses, in distinction from verbal clauses, describe a state. GKC calls subject-predicate the "natural arrangement of words in the noun clause."[62] (141.l) A sort of psycho-linguistic explanation for this is given. GKC holds that the "principle stress" falls on the subject as it is the object being described, and so it appears in the first position.

The reverse order is attributed to various factors.[63] In some instances it is said to be required; such as when special emphasis is put on the predicate, when an interrogative is in the predicate, or with an adjectival predicate. Predicate-subject order is said to be optional when the subject is a pronoun, when the subject consists of several words, or in relative clauses "when the predicate is adverbial or compounded with a preposition." Especially interesting is the brief explanation that GKC gives to situations when the predicate precedes a subject that is an independent personal pronoun. It is said that the personal pronoun, being used of a known person "does not excite the same interest as that which is stated about him" (141.n). When taken together with GKC's rationale for the basic subject-predicate order, one sees that word order is considered dependent on what is the most salient piece of information communicated by an utterance.

---

[60] From this point on GKC will refer to only the 2nd English edition.

[61] Kautzsch, E., ed., *Gesenius' Hebrew Grammar*, trans. A. E. Cowley (Oxford: Clarendon, 1910), 451.

[62] Ibid., 454.

[63] Ibid., 454–55.

GKC opens its discussion of verbal clauses highlighting the importance of word order. "There is an essential distinction between verbal clauses, according as the subject stands before or after the verb."[64] The idea of emphasis/stress continues to underlie the presentation of word order. Hebrew is described as having a natural word order of VSO. This is because in a verbal clause the primary emphasis is on the action and so it precedes the subject. GKC gives two categories of reasons for a SV word order. The first is based on the principle of emphasis: when the subject receives some special emphasis, it is fronted. Other elements such as the object can also be fronted for special emphasis. The second type of reason for SV clauses, which represents "the great majority of [SV] instances," is when the clause itself does not carry the narrative forward. Such clauses instead, much like nominal clauses, describe a state.[65] Such states can be acts completed before the principal action of the narrative, and are supplied as explanatory material. They can also be contemporaneous with the principal events or existing because of them. Therefore, GKC subsumes the categories employed by later grammarians for the "offline" nature of many SV clauses (circumstantial, explanatory, parenthetical, etc.) under the unifying category of "describing a state."

2.3.2. Waltke/O'Connor (1990)

Introduction to Biblical Hebrew Syntax (IBHS) has surprising little to say about word order. IBHS dedicates a significant section to word order in nominal clauses (8.4). This section follows Andersen. The "basic relation" which acts as a key to BH is the order governing-governed.[66] Word order in verbal clauses is only treated in the

---

[64] Ibid., 455.

[65] Ibid. GKC mentions that sometimes in cases when the verbal from could be read as a participle it very well could have been that the writer intended a nominal clause.

[66] Bruce Waltke and M. O'Connor, *An Introduction to Biblical Hebrew Syntax* (Winona Lake, IN: Eisenbrauns, 1990), 52–53.

section devoted to nominative functions in the noun system (8.3.b).[67] All other comments about word order are relegated to notes, from which the following can be gleaned.

BH has VS as its basic word order. This word order "usually obtains" in clauses with no introductory material, with *wayyiqtols*, or with adverbial clauses (8.3.b).[68] SV word order is the normal word order following a disjunctive waw. Section 39.2.3 treats the disjunctive waw, which is defined as "an interclausal waw before a non-verb constituent."[69] The disjunctive roles discussed in the section are explicitly connected with the waw and not the word order. However, due to the connection between the disjunctive waw and SV word order, one can also conclude that the SV word order itself has a disjunctive function. In line with the study of de Regt,[70] IBHS states that Hebrew (in contrast to many other languages) does not have a varying basic word order between main and subordinate clauses.[71]

2.3.3. Davidson/Gibson (2000)

J. C. L. Gibson has revised Andrew Davidson's *Hebrew Syntax* (DG). The present version interacts with word order at numerous places throughout the grammar. DG distinguishes between nominal and verbal word order according to the modern definition. However, he also recognizes and interacts with the Arabic definition.[72]

For nominal clauses, DG follows Andersen, but notes four exceptions from the SP = identifying and PS=classifying schema.[73]

---

[67] Ibid., 129.

[68] Ibid.

[69] Ibid., 650.

[70] Lénart J. de Regt, "Word Order in Different Clause Types in Deuteronomy 1–30," in *Studies in Hebrew and Aramaic Syntax Presented to Professor J. Hoftijzer on the Occasion of His Sixty-Fifth Birthday*, ed. K. Jongeling, H. L. Murre-van den Berg, and L. Van Rompay (New York: Brill. 1991), 152–72.

[71] Waltke and O'Connor, *Introduction*, 635.

[72] J. C. L. Gibson ed., *Davidson's Hebrew Syntax* (Edinburgh: T&T Clark, 2000), 54.

[73] Ibid., 52–53.

These are described as "syntactic structures which override these patterns."[74] The first is that nominal circumstantial clauses behave like
verbal circumstantial clauses and begin with the subject, so when a
nominal circumstantial clause is classifying it will still be SP. The second is that constructions presenting two contrasting subjects will have
both subjects begin their respective clauses. The third is when the pattern overridden in order to serve the creation of a chiasm. The final
exception is when classifying clauses contain the word כֹּל, which is
said to usually come first.[75]

DG describes the the normal order of the verbal clause as VS
followed by the rest of the predicate.[76] In earlier sections, DG describes the relative placement of indirect and direct objects as
IO-DO.[77] This results in a usual VS-IO-DO order. DG notes that "the
long YIQTOL, espec. in prose, tends to avoid the initial position."[78]

DG comments that whenever an item is fronted before the
verb, it is receiving some sort of "emphasis." Although he goes on to
say that this is an insufficient way to describe alternative word orders.
For DG, alternative word orders have syntactic functions on two orders—macrosyntactic and microsyntactic. DG's terminology is not
widely used or obviously transparent. For DG, syntactic functions op-
erate on relationships outside the bounds of their own claus-
es/sentences. When DG says "syntactic," he means that a word order
within a particular clause is signaling something about that clause as a
whole and its relationship to the wider context. The more usual term
for such functions would be discourse and pragmatic functions.

DG's macrosyntactic functions include signaling structure and
making offline remarks in a narrative. When subjects precede verbs,

---

[74] Ibid., 53.

[75] Ibid., 53.

[76] Ibid., 164.

[77] Ibid., 108–14.

[78] *Long YIQTOL* is how DG refers to the "imperfect" prefixed conjugation
as distinct from "short YIQTOL" form which underlies the morphology of the jus-
sive/*wayyiqtol* conjugations.

this sometimes signals that the sentence in question is the beginning of a new episode in a narrative. Additionally, DG holds that all clauses (with few exceptions) that give circumstantial information are signaled with the subject first. Microsyntactic is used to describe the signaling of relationships between clauses in compound/complex sentences, such as conveying similarity or contrast. A subject or object might be fronted in the second half of a complex sentence in order to contrast it with a subject or object in the first half. DG concludes that the normal word order should really be regarded as the unmarked word order. That is to say, it is the word order that is employed when one of the macro- or microsyntactic functions is not being employed.

2.3.4. Merwe/Naudé/Kroeze (2002)

A Biblical Hebrew Reference Grammar (MNK) concludes with an entire chapter on word order. MNK notes that BH has often been described as a VSO language due to the statistical dominance of verb first clauses. This statistical dominance is ascribed to two factors: (1) Person, number, and gender in the *qatal* and *yiqtol* are marked in the verbal conjugation itself and not with an independent personal pronoun, and (2) *weqatal* and *wayyiqtol* forms require a verb first word order. Given a VSO normal word order, whenever a constituent precedes the verb, that word order is considered marked.[79]

MNK seeks to provide "a more nuanced" view of word order that (1) gives a more detailed explanation of fronted constituents rather than to simply attribute them to "emphasis" and (2) accounts for word order variation in the area of the clause following the verb (what MNK calls the main field).[80] In order to accomplish giving this more nuanced view, MNK gives a series of important considerations. The most relevant for our present study are the distinction between the preverbal and main fields, the multiple functions that fronting can have, and the distinction between when a word order is obligatory and when the au-

---

[79] Christo H. J. van der Merwe, Jackie A. Naudé, and Jan H. Kroeze, *Biblical Hebrew Reference Grammar* (Sheffield: Sheffield Academic, 1999), 336.

[80] The latter is beyond the scope of this book.

thor had a choice in how they ordered the constituents.[81]

By distinguishing between obligatory word order and word orders that represent a choice by the speaker, MNK provides a more functional description of what is marked and what is unmarked. An obligatory word order is not truly a marked word order, because there is no option to use an unmarked word order. MNK further distinguishes between obligatory constituents in the preverbal field and those elements that should be considered part of the verbal field (e.g., negatives and "emphatic" infinitive absolutes).[82] Words that are part of the verbal field are not considered fronted. The unmarked order of verbal clauses is Verb - Subject - Object - Indirect Object - Prepositional Object - other complement/adjunct - complement/adjunct(place) - complement/adjunct(time).[83]The unmarked order of nominal clauses is subject-predicate.[84] Fronting is moving any of the post-verbal constituents into the pre-verbal position.[85]

True fronting has "semantic-pragmatic" functions. MNK relates these functions to the ideas of topic and focus. MNK notes that cross-linguistically, utterances with the predicate as the focus are the "most unmarked." From this, it follows that VSO (as the unmarked order) in BH communicates a predicate focus. Fronting is usually used to depart from this in some way. The primary functions of fronting in BH are (1) indicate that an entity is the focus of an utterance; (2) introduce, activate, or reactivate an entity as the topic of an utterance; (3) signal the use of the anterior construction; and (4) signaling simultaneous or near simultaneous actions.[86]

When an entity is made the focus of an utterance, this can be done for any number of reasons. Included in this category would be

---

[81] Ibid., 337.

[82] Ibid., 338–40.

[83] Ibid., 342.

[84] Ibid., 343.

[85] MNK further discusses movement in the main field. Salient movement in that case is away from the verb (*Biblical Hebrew Reference Grammar*, 342–43). Further treatment of mainfield movement will not be featured in this book.

[86] Ibid., 346–50.

instances when answers to questions are fronted. Fronting used to
mark the topic is also used in multiple situations. The fronted constituent could be introduced for the first time as a new topic, such as at the
start of a new episode. The fronting can also occur to reactivate a previously known topic.

2.3.5. Arnold/Choi (2003)

A Guide to Biblical Hebrew Syntax (GBHS) covers word order
in its section on clauses. GBHS distinguishes between verbal and
nominal clauses as most others do. Nominal clauses are treated following Andersen. Verbal clauses are described as having the typical
word order of VSO, with temporal emphasis (any temporal particle or
phrase) coming before the verb.[87] Six reasons are given for the departure from the typical order: (1) the subject will precede the verb for
emphasis, (2) the subject will precede the verb when there has been a
change in subject, (3) the object may precede the verb for emphasis,
(4) the essential part of the reply to a question will come first, (5) poetic variation for style, and (6) interrogatives precede the verb.[88] It is
not clear why interrogatives are treated as a departure from typical
word order. GBHS provides four pragmatic reasons for departure from
typical word order. The most defined being the use of alternative word
orders to front/emphasize the essential part of the reply to a question.

2.3.6. Williams/Beckman (2007)

Williams' Hebrew Syntax (WB) is a new edition of Ronald
Williams' *Hebrew Syntax: An Outline*, revised by John C. Beckman. It
includes an entire section on word order; covering both the word order
in verbal and nominal clauses. Beckman describes the presentation as
"a traditional analysis of the topic."[89] A wide bibliography of word
order studies is provided initially, but most of the actual references in

---

[87] Bill T. Arnold and John H. Choi, *A Guide to Biblical Hebrew Syntax*
(Cambridge: Cambridge University Press, 2003), 169.

[88] Ibid., 169–70.

[89] John C. Beckman ed., *William's Hebrew Syntax: Third Edition* (Toronto:
University of Toronto Press, 2007), 201.

the body of the section are from GKC, JM, MNK, IBHS and Katsuomi Shimasaki's study.

In keeping with the general format of the rest of the book, the section on word order is a bullet-point list, with examples of various word orders that one encounters in BH. WB states that the basic order of verbal clauses is VSO followed by any adverbial or prepositional phrases.[90] WB provides nineteen other points following this statement. Each bullet point either only describes a particular word order situation or describes and gives a pragmatic reason for a particular word order.[91]

A good representative example of the former is point 572e, "A preposition with a pronominal suffix may precede the subject."[92] No elaboration on any difference between this construction and having the prepositional phrase follow the subject is given. A good example of when a pragmatic explanation is supplied is point 573a, "The subject may precede the verb to focus attention on the subject."[93]

These nineteen points can also be divided between those that WB considers normative and those that are considered exceptions to BH's typical word order. The exceptions can be recognized based on the consistent way WB refers to them. All "deviant" word orders are described with the word "may," e.g., "A subject *may* precede a verb."[94] Deviant word orders that are given pragmatic functions can be summarized as occurring to indicate focus, contrast, simultaneous or anterior time, change of subject, or for reasons of poetic style. Among the situations that are considered part of the regular word order are expressions of time, negatives, and interrogatives preceding the verb, as well as inverted word order in clauses that adverbially function to describe the manner of the action of the main clause. WB's section on word order in nominal clauses follows Andersen.[95]

---

[90] Ibid.

[91] Ibid., 202–8.

[92] Ibid., 202.

[93] Ibid., 203.

[94] Ibid., 203; see many examples on this page.

[95] Ibid., 206–8.

2.3.7. *Joüon/Muraoka (2011)*

Takamitsu Muraoka's revision of Paul Joüon's *A Grammar of Biblical Hebrew* (JM) labels verb-subject as the unmarked word order in verbal clauses. This unmarked status is correlated with statistical dominance.[96] This is a departure from the original French version of Joüon's grammar as Muraoka mentions in a note on the introductory section covering clauses.[97] In the sections following the identification of VS as unmarked, JM lists various types of clauses, notes their usual word order, and gives an account of exceptions to the unmarked word order.[98]

Clauses that exhibit VS word order include those with interrogatives, jussives, and verbal clauses with a particle. Negative particles usually come first and word order will be determined based on which element the negation relates to. If the negation is meant to rule out the subject as the performer of the action, then the word order will be SV. If the negation is meant to say that the subject did not perform a particular action, then the word order will be VS. Clauses with a particle also often place a special emphasis on the subject, in which case the SV order is used.

Word order for clauses that begin with a waw is dependent on form.[99] Any clause with a *weqatal* or *wayyiqtol* will necessarily be VS when an explicit subject is included. In some cases, the waw must be separated from the verb, and the order is SV (otherwise called the dis-

---

[96] Paul Joüon and T. Muraoka, *A Grammar of Biblical Hebrew* (Roma: Gregorian & Biblical Press, 2011), 545. "The statistically dominant and unmarked word order in the verbal clause is: Verb-Subject." It is not clear what relationship between statistically dominant and unmarked is meant. It could be that the statistical dominance is what necessitates the judgment of VS order as "unmarked" or that the unmarked status of VS is what results in its statistical dominance.

[97] Ibid., 525; "Indeed, some authorities hold that in both types of clause the normal word order is Subject-Predicate." Muraoka goes on to cite the original French version of Joüon's grammar.

[98] Ibid., 545–51.

[99] Ibid., 546.

junctive waw). Such separation may be necessary to "indicate the absence of sequence."[100]

Cases where the SV word order will appear include emphasizing or contrasting the subject, creating a circumstantial clause, at the beginnings of statements,[101] when the subject is an answer to a question asked, for poetic/stylistic reasons, and possibly in order to front "God" for religious purposes. JM observes that circumstantial clauses and those at the beginning of statements do not seem to place any special emphasis on any of the constituents and usually have SV word order.[102]

2.4. Summary

Most of the grammars, whether they use the terminology or not, can be summarized using a few key linguistic concepts. They treat BH word order variation as having a pragmatic, discourse, and/or semantic function. Pragmatic functions include the marking of constituents as having a specific role in the clause. Discourse functions include marking the clause as having a particular relationship to the surrounding clauses. Semantic functions would include the identification of verbs as having an irrealis mood.

In order to navigate the various proposals for BH word order, it is necessary to have a unified vocabulary and theoretical framework. With this in mind, the next chapter will introduce and define the major linguistic concepts that have been encountered in this survey of the BH literature. Only with these definitions in place can we truly understand the proposals found in Chapter 4.

---

[100] Ibid.

[101] By "the beginning of statements" JM means the start of new episodes or sub-episodes.

[102] Ibid., 525–26.

Chapter 3
LINGUISTIC FOUNDATIONS

The issue of word order typology can be put in the form of a question: What is a language's basic word order? Basic word order has received multiple definitions in linguistic literature. In Hebrew studies it is often left undefined. Possible ways to define basic word order include: the word order most often encountered in a language, the word order from which other word orders are derived, or the word order that signals no special functions.

Chapter 2 has shown that BH has most often been classified as a VSO language. Unfortunately, much of the word order discussion in commentaries based on this conclusion is vague to the point of being unhelpful.[1] This is epitomized in what is perhaps the most common descriptor for fronted constituents—"emphasis." Randall Buth observes that "one does not need to read much text before discovering that emphasis is a misleading nomenclature for fronted constituents, yet a reader cannot just throw up hands in despair and treat word order functions as unrecoverable."[2] Careful linguistic study provides the opportunity to be more exact in describing the function of word order variation in BH.

In order to interact with the representative positions on word order in BH, this chapter will be devoted to introducing the linguistic concepts that have shaped the study of word order in BH scholarship. The major concepts are discourse-analysis and pragmatics. It is only after a proper discussion of these fields that basic word order can be defined and examined.

---

[1] In my survey of Genesis commentaries, I found only a few that made direct comments on word order in my sample corpus. What discussion did appear was sparse.

[2] Randall Buth, "Word Order in the Verbless Clause," 96.

3.1. Discourse-Analysis

The most obvious function for word order in English is to mark syntactic roles within a sentence, e.g., subject, object, etc.

(1) Bill hit the car.

(2) The car hit Bill.

Word order in these two examples is the only way to differentiate between two possible propositions.[3] In considering cases like this, the question of word order and function remains with the realm of the individual sentence. The difference between a subject and an object can be illustrated within a single sentence. Older linguistic definitions of grammar centered on the formation of the sentence. "It is evident that the sentences in any utterance are marked off by the mere fact that each sentence is an independent linguistic form, *not included by virtue of any grammatical construction* in any larger linguistic form."[4] [emphasis mine]

However, one must move beyond the sentence level if one is to comprehend all the functions of word order variation.[5] Teun A. van Dijk has argued that it is impossible to account for the various sentence shapes a particular utterance might take by only describing each sentence in isolation.[6] If this is true then one must recognize linguistic units that are composed of multiple sentences. In that case those sentences are connected by grammatical constructions.

---

[3] Pamela Downing, "Word Order in Discourse: By Way of Introduction," in *Word Order in Discourse*, ed. Pamela Downing and Michael Noonan (Amsterdam: Benjamins, 1995), 9.

[4] Leonard Bloomfield, *Language* (Chicago: University of Chicago Press, 1933), 170.

[5] Downing, "Word Order in Discourse," 9–17; Downing discusses at least eight functions of word order beyond conveying propositional content.

[6] Teun A. van Dijk, *Text and Context. Explorations in the Semantics and Pragmatics of Discourse* (New York: Longman Group, 1982), 3.

3.1.1. Operating on a Level Above the Sentence

Discourse-analysis (also known as text-linguistics[7] and narra-tive-syntax[8]) is the linguistic discipline that seeks to identify and for-mulate rules in a particular language that govern the construction of a discourse or text. In this book, the use of the term discourse is meant to refer to stretches of language communication longer than a sentence. This can be visualized as a level of communication above the sentence. Discourse can be broadly defined as a series of sentences unified by any outside constraint. Cotterell and Turner define it as "any coherent sequence of strings, any coherent stretch of language."[9] A discourse might be as short as a paragraph or as long as a novel. The terms dis-course and text will be used interchangeably in this book.[10]

Longacre says that the goal of discourse analysis is "to con-front the morphosyntax of a language with the structure of texts in that language to the mutual elucidation of both."[11] The goal is to produce a grammar that accounts for the ways particular morphological units, words, and structures are used and related across sentences in order to aid in the construction of a mental representation of the intended

---

[7] *Text-Linguistics* is more commonly used outside of the United States.

[8] See Christo van der Merwe, "An Overview of Hebrew Narrative Syntax," in *Narrative Syntax and the Hebrew Bible: Papers of the Tilburg Conference 1996*, ed. E. J. van Wolde (Leiden: Brill. 1997), 120.

[9] Peter Cotterell and Max Turner, *Linguistics and Biblical Interpretation* (Downers Grove, IL: InterVarsity Press, 1989), 230.

[10] Michael Stubbs notes that some uses of the terms 'discourse' and 'text' have oppositional nuances, "First, one often talks of *written text* versus *spoken dis-course*. Or alternatively *discourse* often implies *interactive discourse*; whereas *text* implies *non-interactive monologue*, whether intended to be spoken aloud or not." Michael Stubbs, *Discourse Analysis* (Chicago: University of Chicago Press, 1983), 9. I follow Stubbs (and others such as van Dijk, *Text and Context*, 3; and Cotterell and Turner, *Linguistics and Biblical Interpretation*, 230) in avoiding such nuances and speaking of 'text' and 'discourse' synonymously.

[11] Robert Longacre, "Some Hermeneutic Observations on Textlinguistics and Text Theory in the Humanities," in *Functional Approaches to Language, Culure, and Cognition: Papers in Honor of Sydney M. Lamb*, ed. David G. Lock-wood, Peter H. Fries, and James E. Copeland (Amsterdam: Benjamins, 2000), 170.

communicated information.

A discourse is more than simply a series of sentences. Any series could be viewed as a random mess or a unified whole. In order for a series of sentences to convey a unified meaning the series needs to have coherence. Van Dijk defines coherence as "a semantic property of discourses, based on the interpretation of each individual sentence relative to the interpretation of other sentences."[12] However, it is better to nuance further and say that coherence, being a conceptual mental framework, is not a property of texts or discourses themselves, but what a particular reader at any given moment is able to do with a text. "A text is said to be COHERENT if, for a certain hearer on a certain hearing/reading, he or she is able to fit its different elements into a single overall mental representation."[13]

The fact that coherence is to be located in the mind of the recipient does not mean that texts and languages do not use specific and concrete linguistic signals in order to facilitate coherence. The use of such linguistic signals is called cohesion.[14] Individual languages all have unique means for linking sentences and propositional content over extended discourses. These means are properly an area of study in any language's grammar and are the purview of discourse-analysis.

Not only is it possible to analyze the means by which a language uses linguistic signals to produce coherence, it is necessary for a successful description of grammatical phenomena in any language. Longacre in 1979 wrote of the need for discourse-level grammar.

> It is not simply that systematic analysis and study of units larger than the sentence is possible, nor even that such an analysis is desirable, but rather that discourse analysis is a rock bottom necessity, i.e., all linguistic structure must ultimately be related to the structure of the context.[15]

---

[12] van Dijk, *Text and Context*, 93.

[13] Robert A. Dooley and Stephen H. Levinsohn, *Analyzing Discourse: A Manual of Basic Concepts* (Dallas: SIL International, 2001), 23–24.

[14] Ibid., 27–34.

[15] Robert Longacre, "Why We Need a Vertical Revolution in Linguistics,"

He surveys a number of areas that cannot be adequately described if one is operating only at the level of the sentence.[16] Three examples suffice to illustrate: pronouns/deictics, voice, and stress variation in English.

The choice between deictic elements in the following English sentences requires a context in order to explain.[17]

(1) A boy ate a cookie.
(2) The boy ate a cookie.

The need for a context is observed in this brief explanation of articles and pronouns,

> ...the definite determiner "the" signals that the information following is already "known" to the speaker and hearer. Pronouns signal that their referents have been previously mentioned, or are readily identifiable in the context of communication or on the basis of the speaker and hearer's mutual knowledge.[18]

In defining the definite article, one must reference a context of usage. Whether one refers to "a boy" or "the boy" is dependent on the current status of the entity in question in the minds of the speaker and the lis-

---

in *Fifth LACUS Forum*, ed. Wolfgang Wolck and Paul L. Garvin (Columbia, SC: Hornbeam, 1979), 249.

[16] Ibid.

[17] My use of context in this book is general in scope, following Stephen C. Levinson, "where the term **context** is understood to cover the identities of participants, the temporal and spatial parameters of the speech event, and (as we shall see) the beliefs, knowledge and intentions of the participants in that speech event, and no doubt much besides." Levinson, *Pragmatics* (Oxford: Oxford University Press, 1987), 5; and Long, *Grammatical Concepts 101 for Biblical Hebrew*, 151. Context includes the concepts denoted in more exact literature by the two terms cotext and context.

[18] James Paul Gee, *An Introduction to Discourse Analysis: Theory and Method* (London: Routledge, 2011), 129.

tener. Such status is only recoverable by looking at the entire discourse.

One also encounters the potential need to appeal to context in order to explain the choice between passive and active voice in English. As many have observed, "[T]here are various morpho-syntactic ways to express the 'same' information about an ordered sequence of facts."[19] An active sentence can be transformed and rendered in the passive voice without changing the proposition.

(3) Dan ate the cookie.

(4) The cookie was eaten by Dan.

Both convey the same propositional content. How can the difference between the uses of either be explained? Longacre notes that often the simplest way to explain the passive voice in English is to relate it to "the need to preserve thematicity in discourse..."[20]

Finally, there is the use of vocal stress (marked by italics) in the following English sentence.

(5) I ate *the cookie*.

In this example the stress is on the direct object. The function and the purpose of this stress cannot be described only in relationship to the sentence itself. Alternatively, the stress could have been put on the subject or the verb. Each alternative would not be suitable in the same discourse contexts. They are not interchangeable within a discourse. "[The] assignment of intonation and stress is impossible to a sentence without taking account of its context."[21] One must move outside the sentence to the wider discourse in order to explain the stress. This utterance could be the answer to a question (What did you eat?) or perhaps correction of a mistaken assumption (Did you like the rice?). In

---

[19] van Dijk, *Text and Context*, 207.

[20] Longacre, "Why We Need a Vertical Revolution in Linguistics," 257.

[21] Ibid., 250.

either case, in order to describe the function of the stress, one must use the context of the utterance.

In discourse-analysis the questions of how sentences are formed in relationship to neighboring sentences, their semantic content, and the overall discourse context, take center stage. The word order proposals in Chapter 4 have all incorporated and are dependent on discourse-analysis to one degree or another.

3.1.2. Discourse Analysis in Biblical Hebrew

The significance of a grammar of BH that operates at a level higher than the sentence is something most students encounter early in their studies. This is true even if the language and terminology of discourse-analysis is not employed. This can be illustrated by the juxtaposition of two simple sentences.

(1) קטל האיש את הסוס

(2) ויקטל האיש את הסוס

In translation, both sentences can be rendered into English:

(3) The man killed the horse.

(1) and (2) convey the same propositional content. However, at this point one recognizes that the further question arises, "When does one use one form in preference to another?"[22] The question for the example is, "What governs the choice between the use of the *qatal* or the *wayyiqtol* verb form?" Are the two verb forms interchangeable? The answer is no, and students are taught to recognize this from the beginning of their BH instruction. In order to answer the question of *qatal* vs *wayyiqtol*, one must look beyond the sentence. This is what students are taught to do in recognizing *wayyiqtol* as the "narrative" form.[23]

The above example should prove the necessity of at least some

---

[22] Ibid., 253.

[23] So many of the grammars surveyed in Chapter 2.

amount of discourse-grammar for BH in order to account for even the most basic grammatical phenomena. It is now a matter of applying discourse level considerations to the task of answering other fundamental questions about BH grammar. In this book discourse considerations are applied to the question of basic word order.

3.2. The Third Linguistic Dimension: Pragmatics

Pragmatics is one of the key fields of linguistic inquiry relevant to a discourse level grammar of word order in BH. In this section, I will define and give examples of pragmatics, and relate it to syntax and semantics. A recognized relationship between the three is as old as pragmatics as a linguistic term.[24] While the concerted pursuit of syntax and semantics as fields of linguistic inquiry has been widespread for some time, adequate and comprehensive discussions of pragmatics has lagged behind.[25] Pragmatics along with syntax and semantics, are what I shall call different dimensions of linguistic description.[26] Pragmatics has recently been the subject of much vigorous study. Even though the introductory BH grammars do not usually devote specific discussions to the pragmatic dimension (Cook/Holmstedt excepted), this third dimension proves to be central to the scholarly discussion of word order phenomena in BH.

Pragmatics has been broadly defined as the study of "language in use."[27] Morris' original definitions of pragmatics, syntax, and se-

---

[24] Yan Huang and Stephen C. Levinson both credit Charles W. Morris with coining the term "pragmatics" and cite his threefold division of semiotics into syntax, semantics, and pragmatics. Yan Huang, *Pragmatics: Oxford Textbooks in Linguistics* (Oxford: Oxford University Press, 2014), 2; and Levinson, *Pragmatics*, 1–2.

[25] Ruth Kempson, "The Syntax/Pragmatics Interface," in *The Cambridge Handbook of Pragmatics,* ed. Keith Allan and Kasia M. Jaszczolt (Cambridge: Cambridge University Press, 2012), 529–30.

[26] Morris also speaks of this triad as "dimensions." Charles W. Morris, "Foundations of the Theory of Signs," in *International Encyclopedia of Unified Science*, ed. O. Neurath, R. Carnap, and C. Morris (Chicago: University of Chicago, 1938), 92.

[27] Huang, *Pragmatics*, 1.

mantics centered around examining specific relationships: Syntax being the study of "formal relations of signs to one another"; semantics
being the study of "the relations of signs to the objects to which the
signs are applicable"; and pragmatics being the study of "the relation
of signs to interpreters."[28] This narrows the scope of what is meant by
"in use" in the broad definition. By "in use" it is meant that pragmatics
is concerned with how language relates to its particular context when
employed. One can further limit the definition to the study of concrete
and identifiable grammatical features that signal these relationships.
For the purposes of this book, I will adopt one of the definitions given
by Stephen C. Levinson: "Pragmatics is the study of those relations
between language and context that are **grammaticalized**, or encoded
in the structure of a language."[29] [emphasis in original]

This definition can now be related to the other two dimensions
of linguistic inquiry.[30] Syntax refers to the construction of a sentence
in a language. In the communicative act the syntactical dimension is
the actual arrangement of the constituents that make up any given sentence in order for them to be sensible. The semantic dimension of the
utterance is the particular propositional content that is encoded and
communicated by the sentence.[31] That provides two dimensions: form
(syntax) and content (semantics).

As an example, imagine that someone has a mental image of a

---

[28] Morris, "Foundations of the Theory of Signs," 91, 99, and 108.

[29] Levinson, 9.

[30] By speaking of "three dimensions" I do not mean to limit linguistic inquiry to these three. The terminology is meant to be a unifying device that "bundles"
the three together for my purposes in the present work.

[31] By speaking of "propositional content" and not "meaning," I am trying to
avoid bundling the areas covered by pragmatics under semantics, as some have done
in the past. This is not a judgment on the philosophy/linguistic methodology of doing
so, but a practical decision to attempt isolate and discuss pragmatic meanings conceptually apart from other types of meaning. For example, Andrew Carnie, *Syntax: A
Generative Approach* (Oxford: Blackwell, 2007), 3–4. Carnie stops at the semantic
level as far his summary of the levels of language is concerned and would presumably include pragmatic concepts in his semantic level.

man riding a horse. In English one could communicate that mental image with the sentence:

(1) A man rode the horse.

The issue of what images and meanings are conveyed by the words "man," "rode," "horse," etc., are the domain of semantics. The necessary arrangement of the words falls under syntax. The particular way the words are arranged (e.g., man preceding verb) convey syntactic relationships (a verb and its relative subject and object) and those syntactic relationships, coupled with their semantic content, convey a particular proposition.

However, there is a third dimension to communication that can be linguistically encoded. That dimension is the relationship between the propositional content and the information already shared or established by the participants in a communication. The sentence above communicates a particular semantic content, but what is the role that content is meant to have in the discourse? In other words, why are we being told about the man and horse? Are there linguistically identifiable ways that such information is signaled? The methods and study of this third dimension are the purview of pragmatics. The three dimensions might be called: form (syntax), content (semantics), and function (pragmatics).

In English there is ample room for the rearrangement of constituents in order to communicate various pragmatic concerns. So one might say,

(2) The horse was ridden by a man.

Semantically (1) and (2) can be said to encode the same propositional content; however, the sentences are not interchangeable. The differences can be explained at the syntax dimension: the constituents occupy varying syntactic roles between sentences. But how does one explain the choice between one or another, given the identical semantic content? Dooley and Levinsohn have helpfully worded the issue: "In all communication the speaker guides the hearer in adding material to his or her mental representation; semantic content relates to *what* is added, whereas discourse-pragmatic structuring relates to *where* it is added and *how* it relates to what is already there."[32] Each differing sentence above, theoretically conveys different pragmatic relationships between the utterance and the context—each guides the listener to incorporating the semantic content in unique ways to their existing mental framework. This framework would have been established in the preceding discourse.

3.2.1. Information Structure and Pragmatics Roles

In linguistics, identifying specific roles that constituents occupy has proven to have much explanatory power. Various differing linguistic roles exist depending on which linguistic dimension is examined. These roles can be related across dimensions. One can speak of pragmatic roles just as they speak of syntactic and semantic roles.[33] Consider the following example.

(1) The cake was eaten by Bob.

Syntactically speaking, "cake" is the subject of the verb. Subject is a syntactic role that identifies the relationship between a noun/noun phrase and the verb. Other syntactic roles include direct object, indirect object, etc. The same semantic content of the above sentence could be communicated in a different way.

(2) Bob ate the cake.

---

[32] Dooley and Levinsohn, *Analyzing Discourse*, 61–62.

[33] See Comrie, *Language Universals and Linguistic Typology*, 62–63; and van Dijk, *Text and Context*, 114. Whereas some linguists prefer to use different terminologies (i.e., they speak of syntactic functions vs semantic roles), others have used been content to use the same term across dimensions; whether it be 'function' or 'role' or some other term. I have used "roles" across all three dimensions, in order to highlight both the similarities and the differences between the three linguistic dimensions.

In this case Bob is now the subject of the verb. Syntactic roles can change without affecting the propositional content.

Semantically speaking, "cake" is the *patient* of the verb. Patient is a semantic role that identifies the relationship between something in the world and an action. The patient is defined as the entity that is affected by the action. The roles relate directly to the real world event being represented by the utterance. Semantic roles do not change, even as syntactic roles can be changed if the sentence is transformed as above.

Pragmatic roles identify relationships between the semantic content and the context of the utterance. Therefore, pragmatic roles require the identification and tracking of roles across a discourse. One can speak of roles for entire utterances, such as "an answer"—an utterance can be an answer to a question. But one can also speak of pragmatic roles for individual constituents. In the case of (1) above, pragmatically one might say that "cake" is what the entire discourse has been about, and can be called the topic. This identification is dependent on a hypothetical context that has not been supplied.

Pragmatic roles can be indicated through various methods by any given language. In linguistic study, information structure is the particular branch of pragmatics that focuses on the ways that languages encode constituents with pragmatic roles, such as topic and focus. For our present study, the types of various pragmatic roles and how they are indicated by word order are the most relevant area of pragmatics and information structure.

3.2.2. Topic, Comment, and Focus

In the linguistic sub-field of information structure, the three most discussed roles of an utterance are that of the topic, the comment, and the focus. Unfortunately, there is a strong disparity in the use of these terms in the literature. In the following sections, I will give a general definition of each for the purpose of laying conceptual groundwork.[34] In Chapter 4, the unique conceptions of topic, comment, and focus presented by Hebraists will be explored.

3.2.2.1. Topic and Comment

The topic of a sentence can be described as that which the sentence is about.[35] The frustrating part of a definition like this is giving a concrete description of the concept of "aboutness." Topic is a pragmatic role. When I say "about," I mean in relationship to the surrounding discourse or situation. Another way to describe the topic is that it is the entity about which the speaker wishes to make a comment.

Sentences can be divided into two pragmatic components: the topic and the comment. A variant terminology for this twofold division is Theme-Rheme. In his analysis of the English language, Vilem Mathesius defines the theme as "what is given by the context" and "what is being commented on." The rheme is the new part of the sentence and the comment.[36] In colloquial terms, the topic is what the speaker speaks about, the comment is that which the speaker says.[37] The topic-comment duo parallels the dual syntactic components of subject-predicate. In fact, one of the earlier terminologies for topic–

---

[34] My "general definitions" are an attempted hybrid between the most commonly used and what I judge to be the clearest definitions in the literature.

[35] Jeanette K. Gundel and Thorstein Fretheim. "Topic and Focus," in *The Handbook of Pragmatics*, ed. Laurence R. Horn and Gregory Ward (Oxford, MA: Blackwell, 2004), 176. This definition is in keeping with the program set by Simon C. Dik, *The Theory of Functional Grammar: Part I: The Structure of the Clause* (Dordrecht: Foris, 1989), 266. Though it may seem obvious, due to the evolution of the term "topic" it must be pointed out that I am using topic as a pragmatic concept only. It has also been defined syntactically as the constituent which is first in the clause, regardless of its pragmatic role.

[36] Vilem Mathesius, *A Functional Analysis of Present Day English on a General Linguistic Basis*, ed. Josef Vachek (The Hague: Mouton, 1975), 156. Some use theme-rheme as synonymous with topic-comment while others have made a clear distinction between the two by using them to refer to very different concepts.

[37] Hebraists who have followed this approach include Christo van der Merwe, "The Function of Word Order in Old Hebrew—with Special Reference to Cases where a Syntagmeme Precedes a Verb in Joshua," *JNSL* 17 (1991): 135.

comment was psychological subject–psychological predicate.[38] But while there can be overlap between the roles assigned in various dimensions, no one role in one dimension must correspond with a given role in another dimension. In other words, the subject of a sentence is not always the topic of that sentence, the predicate is not always the comment, and so on.

In many linguistic discussions, the topic, as the entity about which a comment is made, is equated with given information.[39] Mathesius gives two different articulations of the topic. "Given by context" and "being commented on" are not coterminous. When defined by information status, the topic of an utterance is that part of the utterance which is already established in the discourse or shared world of the speaker and listener and to which the speaker wishes to add information, updating the mental image. Therefore, the topic-comment binary is sometimes called given-new. However, the primary emphasis in the literature is on the concept of "aboutness."[40] In this work I will follow van Dijk and Dooley/Levinsohn and use the terminology topic, with no definite claims about the given or new status of the information that makes up the topic.

3.2.2.2. Focus

Focus has received even less unified treatments in the literature. The working definition that will be used here revolves around the subjective notion of relative importance. Following in the steps of Si-

---

[38] These terms were in use as early as the later half of the nineteenth century. Gundel and Fretheim, "Topic and Focus," 175; They note that the distinction between the two types of predicates (syntactic and pragmatic) has existed for some time though our present terminology was not employed. Others have used "logical predicate" in recognizing a pragmatic role apart from a syntactic one. Yuen Ren Chao spoke of "the *point* of a message." This 'point' is described as the 'logical predicate' and it is observed that it does not always overlap with the grammatical predicate. Yuen Ren Chao, *A Grammar of Spoken Chinese* (Berkeley: University of California Press, 1968), 78–79.

[39] Gundel and Fretheim, "Topic and Focus," 176.

[40] Moshavi, *Word Order*, 32 and 97.

mon Dik, I define the focus as the most important piece of information contained in an utterance.[41] In Dooley and Levinsohn's words, the focus is the part of an utterance that contains "the most salient change to be made in the hearer's mental representation."[42]

Other studies have defined focus in such a way that it overlaps with the concept of comment/rheme.[43] In many cases the focus is defined as the new information in an utterance.[44] I follow Dooley and Levinsohn in recognizing that, while the most important piece of information conveyed by an utterance is usually new and/or contrastive in nature, it is not always so. Therefore, focus defined by relative importance is a more functional, if less exact, definition for my purposes.

Such a definition may make focus seem subjective, detached, as it were, from any specific cognitive status of information. However, the reality is that writers/speakers at times choose to mark cognitively presupposed information as especially salient. A linguistic theory should be capable of accounting for this.[45]

This means that while the focus can be the comment of the topic-comment, it is not necessarily so. In some cases the focus might be only part of the comment, or it might be the topic, or it might be the entire utterance, in which case both the topic and comment would be considered the focus.[46] Consider the following example.

---

[41] This general definition goes back at least to Simon Dik, *Functional Grammar* (Dordrecht: Foris, 1981).

[42] Dooley and Levinsohn, *Analyzing Discourse*, 62.

[43] Gundel and Fretheim, "Topic and Focus," 176.

[44] Gundel calls this type of focus "semantic focus" while Moshavi renames it "informational focus." Jeanette K. Gundel, "On Different Kinds of Focus," in *Focus: Linguistic, Cognitive, and Computational Perspectives*, ed. Peter Bosch and Rob van der Sandt (New York: Cambridge University, 1999), 295–96; and Moshavi, *Word Order*, 35.

[45] Hornkohl, "Pragmatics of the X-Verb Structure," 37.

[46] This observation follows the influential work Knud Lambrecht, *Information Structure and Sentence Form: Topic, Focus, and the Mental Representations*

(1) Husband – "How is my son?"

(2) Wife –"*Your son* is hungry."

In the wife's response "your son" is clearly the topic. It is also the given information. The husband has asked for information about the son and the wife's response acknowledges that topic and makes a comment on it (he is hungry). However, the stress in the wife's response is put on the topic and not the comment. This rhetorical strategy will probably be all too familiar to the reader. By putting the focus on the topic, the husband's paternal relationship to the topic is brought into prominence. The likely purpose of this topic-stress is to guilt the husband for allowing his son to be in a state of hunger. If the focus were placed on the comment as in,

(3) Your son *is hungry*.

the same pragmatic effect is not achieved. In the case of (3) the point is probably to underscore the relative strength of the hunger. Perhaps the son just played in a soccer match. In (2) the point is to underscore the husband's failure. Perhaps the husband had spent too much time playing soccer with another child and forgot about ordering dinner.

This example shows that a speaker/writer can have a purpose in putting a special stress on something other than the comment of an utterance (in this case the topic). This stress can be achieved by word order variation. It is a pragmatic marking and should be termed and described in a systematic way in any comprehensive discussion of the pragmatic dimension. It is a legitimate pragmatic role. Thus recognizing three pragmatic roles (topic, comment, and focus) instead of two (topic and comment/focus) is a more useful approach.

3.2.3. Conclusion

In BH word order studies, it will be seen that representative scholars view one of the primary functions of BH word order variation

---

of Discourse Referents (Cambridge: Cambridge University Press, 1994).

to be for the pragmatic encoding of specific topic and focus values to constituents. Variation from basic word order is a means of facilitating cohesion in BH. This is true regardless of whether BH is VSO or SVO. However, the functions of a particular word order would change, depending on what the true basic word order is.

3.3. Markedness Theory

The final area of linguistic study that needs to be introduced in order to understand the word order debate is markedness theory. Markedness theory originated in the Prague school of linguistics and was originally limited to the description of phonological phenomena.[47] However, markedness theory has since been applied to grammatical and semantic study. The wide usage of markedness terminology has caused many to question whether or not the disparate phenomena covered can be conceptually grouped together.[48] Regardless of whether or not new terminology should be coined, all instances of markedness terminology involve an opposition between two types of features in language—marked and unmarked.

Unmarked structures are those that are considered default or regular. Marked structures have something added. The additional component can be formal or logical.[49] In morphology, the singular noun 'boy' is considered unmarked. The form 'boys' is considered marked by the addition of the pluralizer, 's'. The opposition in markedness is not between opposites, but between regular and restricted.

Some marked and unmarked pairs are mutually exclusive and not interchangeable in an utterance. This means that the use of one vs. another would change the semantic content of the utterance. Other marked and unmarked pairs function as set and subset. In the latter, the marked item is semantically a subset of the unmarked. In such cases,

---

[47] Henning Andersen, "Markedness Theory–The First 150 Years," in *Markedness in Synchrony and Diachrony,* ed. Olga Miseska Tomic (Berlin: Mouton de Gruyter, 1989), 11–44.

[48] Ibid., 11–12.

[49] Ibid., 12–14.

the unmarked construction can be used to convey the same semantic content as the marked construction.

> (1) I gave her a ring.
> (2) I gave her rings.

The singular form "ring" is unmarked in (1). The corresponding plural form in (2) is marked. The semantic opposition in this marked and unmarked pair is in number. In this example, the unmarked option conveys singularity. 'Rings' is not a subset of 'a ring.' The plural form must be used when the speaker wishes to communicate multiple rings were given.

> (3) He killed the lion.
> (4) He killed the lioness.

The generic form 'lion' is unmarked in (3). The form with the 'ess' suffix specifies a female lion and is marked. However, lion is a generic term that can refer to either a male or female animal. Therefore, while (4) is more specific, the same semantic content (someone killed a female lion) can be conveyed by (3). In speaking of markedness, Roman Jakobson referred to this as "the antinomy between the signalization of A and the non-signalization of A. Two signs may refer to the same objective reality."[50] 'Lioness' signals female in (4). 'Lion' does not signal female in (3), but it does not rule a female out. Therefore, 'lion' and 'lioness' can convey the same objective reality. However, the term 'lion' can also be used in opposition to 'lioness' depending on the context.

> (5) The lions stay home, while the lionesses go out hunting.

---

[50] Roman Jakobson, "Structure of the Russian Verb," in *Russian and Slavic Grammar: Studies 1931–1981* (The Hague: Mouton, 1984), 12. Jakobson's original example used the Russian words for donkey and female donkey. I have substituted a comparable English example.

Jakobson noted this type of situation in elaborating on a second antinomy that arises in connection with the first: "...the antinomy between the non-signalization of A and the signalization of non-A. One and the same sign may possess two different meanings."[51] In our case, 'lion' can either refer to an animal without gender specification or specify a male lion and not be interchangeable with 'lioness.' The examples of (3)-(5) show that markedness oppositions are not as simple as "X not Y."

3.3.1. Markedness in Word Order

Some languages are highly restrictive in their possible word orders, and identifying basic word order is relatively straightforward. However, many languages "exhibit more than one order for at least some pairs of elements."[52] When speaking of word order in BH studies, the types of marking that have been discussed are word orders that add a semantic or pragmatic meaning to a sentence. In the case of two possible word orders conveying the same utterance, the issue is which word order would add some form of meaning. Among such types of meanings that can be added is the identification of pragmatic roles such as topic and focus. The oppositions, in this case, are between the signalization of pragmatic/semantic factor X (the marked form) and the non-signalization pragmatic/semantic factor X (the unmarked form). The complicating factor is the fact that sometimes the unmarked structure actually does signal "no pragmatic/semantic factor X," as Jakobson observed with gender marking on nouns. This is something that we need to be mindful of as we navigate the various proposals by BH grammarians.

3.4. Basic Word Order Defined

It is with the groundwork now laid that basic word order can be

---

[51] Ibid., 12.

[52] Matthew S. Dryer "Word Order," in *Language Typology and Syntactic Description Volume 1: Clause Structure*, ed. Timothy Shopen (Cambridge: Cambridge University Press, 2007), 73.

defined for the purpose of this book. Most of the grammars that were surveyed in Chapter 2 do not give a clear definition of basic word order, before attributing a pragmatic function of some sort to alternate word orders. The lack of a clear definition can often be seen in the use of words like 'usual' or 'normal' for a particular word order.[53] A word order can be both the usual word order in a corpus while simultaneously being a marked word order, if there is a reason for the regular use of a particular type of marking.[54] It is apparent that "basic word order" for the grammars has most often meant the "statistically most common" word order.

To say that VSO is the statistically most common word in BH is not disputed. The problem for defining basic as statistically most common, from a linguistic standpoint, is that word orders that deviate from the statistically most common word order are not necessarily marking anything. It is difficult to assign functions to word orders based on deviation from the statistically most common word order. Therefore, studies in the last sixty years or so have refined what is meant by both "normal" and "emphasized." What Cynthia Miller says in regards to verbless clauses is true of all clauses: "[the question of basic word order] cannot be ultimately solved merely by a statistical analysis of the most frequent word order, since it relates to theoretical issues of language typology and pragmatics."[55]

The grammarians that will be surveyed all ascribe pragmatic and/or discourse functions to word orders that vary from the basic order. Which is to say, word orders can vary from the basic word order by fronting particular constituents for the purpose of marking those

---

[53] Matthew S. Dryer observes that the practice of using words like "normal" without an specification of criteria used is the practice of most grammars of various languages. Dryer, "Word Order," 76.

[54] Matthew S. Dryer, "Frequency and Pragmatically Unmarked Word Order," in *Word Order in Discourse*, ed. Pamela Downing and Michael Noonan (Amsterdam: Benjamins, 1995), 119.

[55] Cynthia Miller, "Pivotal Issues in Analyzing the Verbless Clause," in *The Verbless Clause in Biblical Hebrew: Linguistic Approaches*, ed. Cynthia L. Miller (Winona Lake, IN: Eisenbrauns, 1999), 13.

constituents or the entire clause with a particular pragmatic or discourse role that it otherwise would not explicitly have.[56] Therefore, for
the purpose of this book, basic word order should be understood synonymously with the order that can be taken as a pragmatically neutral
order.[57] It is the order that conveys the non-signalization of pragmatic
and/or semantic information that can be conveyed by word order. This
can also be described as the word order that is unmarked.[58] Basic
means the word order that is neutral and does not select any particular
constituent for an explicit pragmatic role.[59]

---

[56] This definition begins with the "basic" order. A similar definition that
starts from the opposite direction, with the marked orders, can be found in Dryer,
"Frequency and Pragmatically Unmarked Word Order," 105–6; Dryer defines basic
order as the default order. It is the order used when no marked order is needed. One
starts by identifying marked orders and their purpose, and the unmarked order is
"most easily characterized as the order that is used elsewhere."

[57] Ultimately, this definition stops short of answering the question how one
should define basic word order. Adjudicating on this issue is outside the scope of this
work. The participants in the BH debate use competing theoretical grammars and at
times different ideas of what characteristics a basic order should have. However,
since all participants in the debate ascribe differing pragmatic functions to word orders, depending on their view of basic word order, they can be fruitfully compared at
the level of pragmatic and semantic differences in readings.

[58] This is how many grammarians understand basic word order. However,
this definition is not without its challenges. Anna Siewierska has argued that in some
cases, the basic grammatical order should be considered a marked order, depending
on the context. Anna Siewierska, *Word Order Rules* (London: Routledge, 1988), 12–
14. This comes back to the debate over what should be called marked. In Siewierska's examples, the basic order is sometimes not the usual order used for other
reasons. In such a case, Siewierska argues that the basic order should be considered
the marked order, since its use would stand out.

[59] Such a definition does not mean that a basic sentence has no pragmatic
roles assigned in the abstract. This is because not all marked-unmarked pairs are
conveying the signalization of A vs. the signalization of non-A. Note that I define the
unmarked order as the one conveying the non-signalization of A and not as the order
conveying the signalization of non-A. Sentences usually have a specific topic and
always have a focus according to the definitions laid out by most. With regard to the
given-new taxonomy, clauses also always have either new, given, or both. However,
not all sentences explicitly mark constituents as filling those roles. This is an exam-

The word order debate being carried out by Holmstedt, Mo-shavi, and Hornkohl can be described as having at least two levels.[60] The first level of the debate is over which word order does not mark any pragmatic values; which word order can be taken as neutral? The second level of the debate is over the specific functions of the marked word orders. What do marked word orders convey and what is the best systematic approach for describing their various functions? The fol-lowing chapter will explore the proposals put forward by these major voices in the debate.

---

ple of the opposition between the signalization of A and the non-signalization of A.

[60] A third level, outside the scope of the present work, would be the debate over which theoretical linguistic framework is best suited for understanding and de-scribing language as a whole.

Chapter 4

THE VSO AND SVO DEBATE:
PROPOSED INFORMATION STRUCTURES

The debate over which word order is basic is the central concern of this book. In the face of two opposing positions, the question asked here is what types of different interpretations will they produce, if any? The next step in answering this question is to give a detailed explanation of the views of the major positions. Fortunately capable expositions of each side are available, though anything approaching an exhaustive study of word order in BH has yet to materialize.

Most grammars have assumed a VSO basic order and many studies proceed with that assumption without giving a clear case for it. However, the VSO proponents treated below have dedicated a significant percentage of their case to rebutting arguments in favor of the SVO position. For these reasons, I will begin with the SVO representative, Robert Holmstedt, so that the debate can be most easily followed here.[1]

---

[1] The debate in view here is over the typology of what is called Early BH (EBH), Archaic BH (ABH) or Standard BH (SBH). For a succinct summary of the scholarly work on diachronic classifications of BH in the Bible, see Dong-Hyuk Kim, "Linguistic Dating of Biblical Hebrew Text: A Survey of Scholarship," in *Early Biblical Hebrew, Late Biblical Hebrew, and Linguistic Variability: A Sociolinguistic Evaluation of the Linguistic Dating of Biblical Texts* (Leiden: Brill, 2013), 11–43. For an overview of the current state of scholarship on this issue see the essays in Cynthia L. Miller-Naudé and Ziony Zevit eds., *Diachrony in Biblical Hebrew* (Winona Lake, IN: Eisenbrauns, 2012). Modern Hebrew is universally classified as an SVO language. Holmstedt assumes an original VSO structure for pre-Biblical Hebrew. Robert Holmstedt, "Investigating the Possible Verb-Subject to Subject-Verb Shift in Ancient Hebrew: Methodological First Steps," *KUSATU* 15 (2013): 3–31. There is an unquestioned drift from VSO to SVO. In one sense the question is, how early did this drift occur? Talmy Givón argues that the EBH books of Genesis, Joshua, and Judges evidence VSO compared with an SVO preference evidenced in the Late BH books of Esther, Ecclesiastes, Song of Songs. Talmy

4.1. SVO–Robert Holmstedt

Robert Holmstedt approaches BH word order from a generative perspective/theory of linguistics. According to this linguistic theory, sentences are generated by subconscious procedures. Syntactical study in the generative perspective seeks to codify these procedures into rules of sentence production.[2] Such rules, if successfully identified, would be able to produce all grammatical sentences in a language, and only grammatical sentences. Holmstedt has argued at length in many places that BH has a basic word order of SV, from which other word orders are derived.[3] In the following sections, I will summarize Holmstedt's arguments for the basic word order of BH and introduce the information structure that he proposes.[4]

Givón, "The Drift from VSO to SVO in Biblical Hebrew: The Pragmatics of Tense-Aspect," in *Mechanisms of Syntactic Change*, ed. Charles N. Li (Austin: University of Texas Press, 1977), 184–254. Randall Buth has challenged this in "Functional Grammar," 81–82.

[2] See Carnie, *Syntax*, 5–6. Generative grammatical theories have come to dominate linguistics. They have gone by many names (transformational grammar, standard theory, government and binding theory, minimalism, etc) but they go back to the work of Noam Chomsky. See Lyda E. LaPalombara, *An Introduction to Grammar: Traditional, Structural, and Transformational* (Cambridge, MA: Winthrop, 1976), 209–15. The work that is said to have sparked the whole paradigm shift from earlier linguistic theories is Noam Chomsky, *Syntactic Structures* (The Hague: Mouton, 1957).

[3] For works where Holmstedt lays out his case see "The Relative Clause in Biblical Hebrew: A Linguistic Analysis" (PhD Diss., University of Wisconsin-Madison, 2002), 126–59; "The Typological Classifications of the Hebrew of Genesis: Subject-Verb or Verb-Subject?" *JHebS* 11 (2011): 1–39; "Word Order and Information Structure in Ruth and Jonah: A Generative-Typological Analysis," *JSS* 54.1 (2009): 111–39; "Word Order in the Book of Proverbs," in *Seeking out the Wisdom of the Ancients: Essays Offered to Honor Michael V. Fox on the Occasion of His Sixty-Fifth Birthday*, ed. R. L. Troxel, K. G. Friebel, and D. R. Magary (Winona Lake, IN: Eisenbrauns, 2005), 135–54.

[4] The clearest presentation of Holmstedt's argument for a basic SVO order is found in "Typological Classifications of the Hebrew of Genesis." The most thorough explanation of his current information structure is found in "Word Order and Information Structure in Ruth and Jonah." The fullest treatment of his generative-typological approach and the minimalist program from which he operates is still

4.1.1. Holmstedt on Basic Word Order

Holmstedt has identified four criteria that have been used to identify basic word order within languages: frequency, clause type, distribution, and pragmatics. The criteria are not independent of each other and often intersect at important points. Additionally, on their own they each have inherent weaknesses. Holmstedt concludes that these four criteria are to be used together in order to be most fruitfully employed. The identification and careful application of these four have arguably been Holmstedt's most important contribution to this debate.

4.1.1.1. Frequency

In his most recently published works on the topic, Holmstedt has given frequency as the base criterion, which must then be filtered through the others in order to give a meaningful result. The general idea behind the frequency criteria is that the word order that occurs the most in a language is the basic word order. Frequency has been definitional of what many past authors have meant by "basic." Many of the introductory grammars have not made specific claims about typological word order so much as they have made claims about the frequency of certain word orders.

The problems with using frequency as the only criterion or as the definition of a language's "basic word order" are numerous. The most obvious is that what would be considered basic word order could change depending on the size and nature of the sample corpus. A language that has a relatively free word order experiences much variation by definition. This means that it is possible to have a sample corpus dominated by a variant word order for one reason or another. It is fine to observe that VS is statistically dominant in BH, but this does not mean that it is pragmatically neutral. Furthermore, in free order languages sometimes the statistics are not so clear. Holmstedt has rightly questioned, at what ratio of VS to SV or vice versa can one decide that a language should be classified one or the other?[5]

---

to be found in his 2002 dissertation.

[5] Holmstedt, "Word Order in the Book of Proverbs," 145.

4.1.1.2. Distribution

The criterion of distribution says that given two or more options for a given construction, the construction that occurs in the most varied environments must be the basic construction.[6] This is because the construction that occurs in less varied environments is limited and must be tied to the environments where it does occur. This criterion has clear overlap with the recognition that basic clauses are theoretically suited for any situation. The use of a marked construction represents an authorial choice.

Distribution is not the same as frequency, because the issue is the number of possible environments, not the number of occurrences. Theoretically, given two constructions, one construction might be the most frequently occurring in a corpus, yet be the more limited of the two when it comes to the types of environments in which they occur. For the issue of BH word order, each clause representative of either VS or SV order must be examined in light of the clausal type, discourse situation, and other contextual factors in order to determine if one word order is constrained to appear in certain circumstances and if one word order is more free.

This criteria provides the foundation for Holmstedt's exclusion of *wayyiqtol* clauses from consideration of basic word order.[7] Holmstedt points out that the *wayyiqtol* form is limited to specific syntactic environments. The *wayyiqtol* must be verb first. It never allows constituents to precede it (with one possible exception).[8] Any clauses with a *wayyiqtol* cannot be considered basic. This does not mean that the VSO order that *wayyiqtols* exhibit cannot be considered basic, but that the *wayyiqtol* clauses themselves are not examples of a basic clause. Something is operating on them to constrain their word order. Therefore, the *wayyiqtol* as a clause type is not a basic clause.

---

[6] Holmstedt, "Typological Classification," 9.

[7] Holmstedt, "Typological Classification," 9–13.

[8] Ibid., 12. Holmstedt notes that only temporal prepositional phrases may come before it, but he recognizes that there is debate over whether such elements should be considered part of the same clause as the *wayyiqtol*.

4.1.1.3. Clause Type

Holmstedt maintains that "languages often exhibit different word order patterns in different clause types."[9] Most of the grammars surveyed above distinguish between the word order of verbal and nominal clauses. Other types of clause oppositions that might experience word order variation include narrative vs direct speech, independent vs subordinate clauses, and indicative vs irreal clauses.[10] It becomes necessary to identify a particular clause type as that which conveys the basic order of a language. Once this is done, the initial results tallied according to the frequency criteria can be sifted to remove all types of clauses that do not qualify.

Holmstedt has followed Anna Siewierska in identifying "basic" clauses as those that are "stylistically neutral, independent, indicative clauses with full noun phrase (NP) participants, where the subject is definite, agentive and human, the object is a definite semantic patient, and the verb represents an action, not a state or an event."[11] Siewierska's definition begins where others ended in defining basic word order—stylistically neutral. However, her definition also includes a number of other limitations that other Hebraists have objected to.[12]

4.1.1.4. Pragmatics

Holmstedt has pointed out that the pragmatic question is something that must be thoughtfully applied to the issue of determining a language's basic word order. If language were clinically easy to examine, one might hope that this would not be the case. An ideal situation might have a researcher able to make a simple judgment about basic word order and then be free to study the pragmatic reasons for variation in that word order. One could hope to start with a basic word order of BH, in order to examine most accurately the pragmatic concerns of variation from that order. However, the linguistic study of any

---

[9] Holmstedt, "Typological Classification," 13.

[10] Holmstedt, "Typological Classification," 14–20.

[11] Anna Siewierska, *Word Order Rules,* 8.

[12] Such as Moshavi and Hornkohl who are treated below.

language, let alone a dead language with such a limited corpus, is never so neat.

In order to judge whether a word order is basic it is important to evaluate whether or not the word order in question is motivated by pragmatic concerns. The pragmatic criteria for word order says that a language's basic word order is the one that is not the result of any pragmatic marking—neutral clauses give the basic word order. Clauses that are pragmatically marked often have variant word orders (such an observation is the foundation of this and most other BH word order studies). In a real sense there exists a frustrating epistemological circle—one is able to recognize pragmatically marked word orders when basic word order is known, but in order to determine basic word order one must know which word orders are marked.

In order to apply this criteria, clauses with specific word orders must be examined in context, to see if it is plausible that they are marked pragmatically. This means that one way of deciding between an SV or VS order for BH is to examine explicit SV clauses one by one in context to look for indications of a pragmatic marking or whether or not it makes more sense to understand the clause as neutral.[13] The same would be done for VS clauses. An SV word order would not predict for neutral VS clauses and vice versa. The examination of clauses in context for pragmatic motivations for word order has the ability to furnish supporting evidence for one's position.[14]

4.1.2. Holmstedt's Information Structure

When all the criteria are applied, Holmstedt concludes that BH has SV as its basic order. This includes participial clauses, though these are different in that they do not undergo triggered inversion.[15] This

---

[13] As I summarize below, a refined version of this criteria is the most fruitful way of approaching the debate as it stands now.

[14] This is also noted by Aaron Hornkohl in his thesis. He recognizes that the identification of pragmatic motivations for all X-V clauses would be further evidence of the VS view that he proposes. See Hornkohl, "Pragmatics of the X-Verb Structure," 35–122

[15] Holmstedt, "Relative Clause," 157.

basic word order can be changed to VS due to certain syntactic constraints. Furthermore, Holmstedt concludes that clauses with irreal
verbs have VS as the basic order.[16] Any word order movement beyond
semantic (mood oppositions) or syntactic constraints is the result of
movement for pragmatic reasons.

In Holmstedt's proposed information structure of BH, he presents four controlling pragmatic concepts, which are further divided
into two "layers"—theme-rheme and topic-focus.[17] The first layer is
the opposition between the *theme* and the *rheme*. This is comparable to
the given-new opposition.[18] Each clause contains both a theme (that
which is given) and the rheme (that which is new/predicated about the
theme).[19]

According to Holmstedt, BH is a theme-rheme language.[20]
This means that the rheme naturally moves towards the right edge of
the clause and the theme naturally moves towards the left edge.[21] BH

---

[16] Holmstedt, "Relative Clause," 134–43; It is possible to say that verbs can
be "marked for irrealis," by their word order. If such language is used it is important
to note that this marking occurs prior to any movement for pragmatic reasons. A
clause with an irreal verb may have SV order if the subject has been fronted as a
topic or focus. The language that Holmstedt uses is that irrealis "triggers" VS order.

[17] This is a development from Holmstedt's earlier model of information
structure found in his dissertation, "Relative Clause," 200–211. That model had a
three-fold division of key information structure concepts: *theme, rheme,* and *kontrast.* Holmstedt previously desired to avoid the terminological confusion in the literature over *focus* and avoided the term. *Kontrast* is equivalent to *focus* in
Holmstedt's current model discussed here. Holmstedt's current information structure
is said to describe Ruth and Jonah and "may be tested and refined against other,
larger textual units" ("Word Order and Information Structure," 129).

[18] Holmstedt's theme-rheme is comparable to topic-comment or topic-focus
in other treatments. However, Holmstedt also employs topic and focus, but uses them
as distinct categories apart from theme-rheme. Therefore special care must be paid to
terminological differences. As with our definitions in 1.5, Holmstedt defines topic
and focus apart from the concept of given and/or new information.

[19] It is also possible for clauses to contain no theme. In such clauses where
all the information is new, the constituents are all said to be rhematic.

[20] Holmstedt, "Relative Clause," 213.

[21] The terms for the clause edges are based on English, which is a

moves new material to the end of the clause while keeping old information at the front. This natural state of affairs can be disrupted for pragmatic reasons and syntactic constraints.

The primary syntactic constraint in Holmstedt's system is that of triggered inversion.[22] The presence of constituents that are either moved to a position before the subject and verb or that naturally occur before the subject and verb will cause a shift in the usual SV word order. This means that whenever a constituent precedes the verb it triggers an inversion of the normal SV word order to VS. Therefore, the pattern X-VS is the norm.[23]

The second level of Holmstedt's information structure contains the topic and the focus. Though there are some similarities between the use of topic and focus as they have been defined generally, Holmstedt has provided nuanced and detailed definitions that are more concrete.[24] For Holmstedt, the topic is always thematic material (it is always known). The topic functions to select one theme from multiple possible themes. It also can be an element that sets the scene by providing time or place. Therefore topic-fronting would be moving a constituent that is thematic to the front of the clause in order to indicate that it is the topic of the succeeding discourse.[25]

---

left-to-right language. In order to avoid confusion, I have made no change in terminology to the standard scholarly language. This means that for BH, a right-to-left language, the "left edge" of the clause is physically on the right edge of the page (i.e., the beginning of the clause) and vice versa.

[22] Holmstedt, "Relative Clause," 148–50; He observes that such a phenomenon is seen in Modern Hebrew and cannot be ruled out as operative in BH.

[23] This addresses one of Buth's main arguments treated above. Holmstedt draws attention to this fact in "Typological Classification," 28n58.

[24] It is assumed that Holmstedt's definitions are in harmony with the introductory discussion on Topic and Focus in John A. Cook, and Robert D. Holmstedt, *Beginning Biblical Hebrew: A Grammar and Illustrated Reader* (Grand Rapids, MI: Baker Academic, 2013), 114–15 and 127–28. There the definitions for topic and focus are closer to the general definition provided in the present work: "Topics direct the reader very specifically to what the clause is about.... Focus items present contrasts..." (114).

[25] Holmstedt, "Word Order and Information Structure," 126–28.

וַיהֹוָה הֵטִיל רוּחַ־גְּדוֹלָה אֶל־הַיָּם וַיְהִי סַעַר־גָּדוֹל בַּיָּם וְהָאֳנִיָּה חִשְּׁבָה לְהִשָּׁבֵר:
Jonah 1:4

Holmstedt uses Jonah 1:4 as clear illustration of fronting to indicate topic marking in a close span.[26] The fronted topics are under-
lined above. YHWH is fronted as the topic in the first clause of the
verse. The final sentence of the verse switches topics to the ship,
which is fronted. Both YHWH and "the ship" are thematic elements,
already introduced in v. 1 and v. 4 respectively.

If an element is fronted to indicate focus, it is information that
is being contrasted with possible alternatives. These alternatives could
be present in the context of the discourse-world or they can be present
in the minds of the speakers through shared knowledge of the world.
The alternatives do not have to "naturally go together." Holmstedt describes the recognition of these alternatives as the creation of a membership set from which the fronted item is selected.[27]

אֲנִי מְלֵאָה הָלַכְתִּי וְרֵיקָם הֱשִׁיבַנִי יְהוָה לָמָּה תִקְרֶאנָה לִי נׇעֳמִי וַיהוָה עָנָה בִי וְשַׁדַּי הֵרַע
לִי: Ruth 1:21

In Ruth 1:21, the adverb "empty" is fronted to contrast the way
that YHWH brought Naomi back with the way she left ("full").[28] In
this case the alternative is present in the preceding clause. In Ruth 1:17
below, "death" is contrasted with logical alternatives that are not
spelled out explicitly in the text. The clause in question begins with כִּי,
which would act as syntactic trigger, resulting in a VS order. However,
the focus-marking of "the death" fronts it, and results in the surface
SV order.[29]

בַּאֲשֶׁר תָּמוּתִי אָמוּת וְשָׁם אֶקָּבֵר כֹּה יַעֲשֶׂה יְהוָה לִי וְכֹה יֹסִיף כִּי הַמָּוֶת יַפְרִיד בֵּינִי וּבֵינֵךְ:
Ruth 1:17

---

[26] Ibid., 129.

[27] Holmstedt, "Relative Clause," 209.

[28] Holmstedt, "Word Order and Information Structure," 134.

[29] Ibid.

Constituents can be fronted to indicate that they are the topic or a focus. In such cases the normal theme-rheme order can be reversed if part of the rheme is fronted. Furthermore, there can be multiple fronting, such as fronting of both a topic and a focus, or of multiple focuses. The topic of an utterance always comes before the focus. Holmstedt concludes, from his generative perspective the underlying structure relevant to left-fronting can be visualized as **Fig 1**.

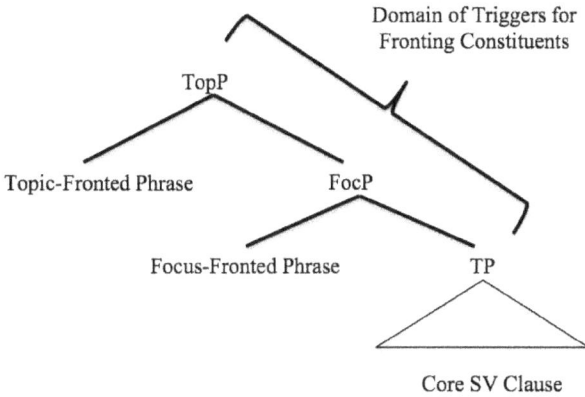

Fig 1. Holmstedt's Pragmatic Structure of a Clause[30]

Constituents are moved into either than TopP or the FocP when they fulfill one of those roles and are fronted in the resultant clause. This means that there can be pragmatic movement that does not affect the surface appearance of the clause. If a subject is moved into the topic or focus slot, the resultant order would still be SVO. Yet the resultant SVO clause is still considered to have a marked constituent.[31] In

---

[30] Reproduced and simplified from Holmstedt, "Word Order and Information Structure," 137; Holmstedt's original graphic included a more complete depiction according to a generative perspective, which involved depicting the level of the clause phrase, which I omitted for simplicity sake.

[31] In the non-generative approaches of other Hebraists there is the recognition that clauses without pragmatic marking still can have a topic and focus. However, 'fronting' is usually only used to describe explicit marking of a topic or focus that deviates from the basic word order. From the VSO perspectives surveyed, in a VSO clause the verb might be the topic and/or focus of the utterance, but it is not considered fronted or marked.

Holmstedt's examination of the books of Ruth and Jonah, he finds only one basic SV clause.[32] All other SV clauses are said to be the result
of topic or focus fronting.[33]

4.2. VSO–Adina Moshavi (2010)

Adina Moshavi wrote her dissertation on pragmatic functions
of the word order of non-subordinate finite clauses in Genesis.[34] This
work was updated and released as *Word Order in the Biblical Hebrew
Finite Clause* (2010). Moshavi 2010 includes data from the larger
corpus of Genesis-2 Kings and an updated response to SVO proponents in which she defends her assumption of a VSO word order.

4.2.1. Moshavi on Basic Word Order

Moshavi begins her discussion by establishing a working definition for basic word order. Two different definitions are discussed—the unmarked/pragmatic definition and the statistically dominant definition.[35] Moshavi adopts the unmarked/pragmatically neutral
definition but recognizes that many others have used the statistically
dominant definition. She acknowledges that "Statistically dominant" is
clearly a less meaningful definition than "pragmatically neutral."[36]
However, most researchers, including Moshavi, still use the frequency
criterion as the backbone of their basic word order argument. In order
to do this, Moshavi relates these two potentially competing definitions
together with the same theoretical understanding of Matthew Dryer.
This framework is still careful to define basic word order as the word
order that is pragmatically neutral, while recognizing the usual statistical dominance of the basic word order. This keeps the two concepts

---

[32] Holmstedt, "Word Order and Information Structure," 129–30.

[33] Ibid., 130.

[34] Adina Moshavi, "The Pragmatics of Word Order in Biblical Hebrew: A
Statistical Analysis" (PhD thesis, Yeshiva University, 2000).

[35] Moshavi also discusses the basic-sentence criterion of Siewierska, but
classifies this as "essentially the pragmatic criterion applied to a small subset of sentence types." Moshavi, *Word Order*, 9.

[36] Moshavi, *Word Order*, 8.

separate but allows them to work together. In this understanding, the attribute of statistically dominant is not definitional or inherent to the concept of basic word order, but it acts as a useful diagnostic of basic word order.[37]

The rest of Moshavi's case consists of establishing the statistical dominance of VSO order and responding to the arguments of SVO proponents. Moshavi cites statistical work by Jongeling, Hornkohl, and herself that establishes the dominance of VSO order. The counts all find that about 80% of clauses with a finite verb are VSO.[38] For Moshavi, "[t]he natural conclusion is that the unmarked position for both subject and object is after the verb."[39] She further argues that VO clauses can even be classified with VSO clauses, "because BH drops pronominal subjects unless they precede the verb..."[40]

In one sense, a key SVO argument can be summarized as "good reasons exist to exclude certain VSO clauses from the counts and when the proper clauses are excluded, SVO is now dominant." It is this line of thinking that Moshavi spends the most time responding to. She reasons that it is improper to exclude *wayyiqtol/weqatal* clauses. She recognizes that if such clauses were marked for a particular semantic or pragmatic factor then it would be wrong to classify them as neutral. She argues that the semantic or pragmatic factor they could be marking is not clear. It cannot be temporal sequentiality due to the occurrences of *wayyiqtols* that are not temporally sequential. A simpler explanation of the form is that it is a "positional variant." This means that the *wayyiqtol/weqatal* is the form used when the word order is

---

[37] Moshavi, *Word Order*, 8; and Matthew S. Dryer, "Frequency and Pragmatically Unmarked Word Order," in *Word Order in Discourse*, ed. Pamela Downing and Michael Noonan (Amsterdam: Benjamins, 1995), 116.

[38] Moshavi, *Word Order*, 11–12; She notes that her study of nonsubordinate clauses in Genesis yields a number of 84% VSO. By her count, Jongeling finds that in Ruth, 20% of clauses with an explicit subject have the subject precede the verb and Hornkohl's examination of both nonsubordinate and subordinate clauses in Genesis results in 79% VSO.

[39] Ibid., 12.

[40] Ibid.

verb first.[41] When in the first position, the verb takes the consecutive form, and such forms should not be excluded from word order counts.

Moshavi also rejects the removal of irreal clauses from the count. She points out that modality is a semantic feature of the verb. A verb can be marked for irrealis without being pragmatically marked. The issue is not whether or not irreal clauses are usually VSO, but whether indicative clauses are usually SVO.[42]

Moshavi's major problem with the application by Holmstedt of Siewierska's basic clause is the "dramatic effect of the basic sentence criterion on text counts."[43] There is an inherent problem that she observes: removing clauses which are considered non-neutral requires that the researcher have some knowledge of which order is marked. She further notes that just because certain contexts are more likely to employ marked constructions, the relative use of marked constructions compared to non-marked constructions is not known.[44] Therefore, while contexts with values that can be pragmatically marked in a language may use such a marked construction, it is not obligatory. It is improper to remove clauses that are possibly marked from consideration. Moshavi concludes that even if one were to remove such clauses, "there is no way to know whether more clauses need to be omitted."[45]

In response to Holmstedt's account of triggered inversion, Moshavi argues that it is not evidence but rather a mechanism that accounts for the widespread existence of VSO clauses. She counters by saying that the surface structure of VSO can be the result of a mandatory inversion in the generative perspective. SVO clauses would then be explained as pragmatically marked.[46] She does not suggest any particular mechanism, but the possibility of the fundamental soundness of the generative theory is left open.

---

[41] Ibid., 12–13.

[42] Ibid., 14.

[43] Ibid., 15.

[44] Ibid.

[45] Ibid.

[46] Ibid., 16.

4.2.2. Moshavi's Information Structure

Moshavi's analysis moves forward on the basis that VSO is the unmarked order, but her study proper is limited to independent finite clauses. She argues that the majority of fronted constituents convey one of two possible pragmatic functions—focusing and topicalization.[47] [48] However, there is a slight asymmetry between the terms as she employs them. While focusing is used to describe fronting a constituent for the purpose of marking it as a focus; topicalization does not refer to the use of fronting to mark a constituent as the topic. Moshavi defines topic using the general "aboutness" definition. For Moshavi, topicalization is by far the majority information structure function used and marks the constituent being topicalized as being in relationship with another constituent in either the immediately preceding or the following context.[49]

4.2.2.1. Topicalization

Moshavi provides helpful elaboration on what it means that topicalization indicates a relationship between constituents. She compares the function of topicalization to discourse connectives.[50] Discourse connectives are words that mark a relationship between clauses

---

[47] Moshavi is following the work of Ellen Prince. For a sample, Ellen Prince, "Topicalization and Left-Dislocation: A Functional Analysis," in *Discourses in Reading and Linguistics*, ed. S.J. White and V. Teller (New York, New York Academy of Sciences, 1984), 213–25; and "Fancy Syntax and Shared Knowledge," *Journal of Pragmatics* 9 (1985): 65–81; and "On the Limits of Syntax, with Reference to Left-Dislocation and Topicalization," in *The Limits of Syntax*, ed. Peter Culicover and Louise McNally (Leiden, Brill, 1988), 288; and Ellen Prince and Gregory Ward, "On the Topicalization of Indefinite NP's," *Journal of Pragmatics* 16 (1991): 161–77.

[48] Moshavi, *Word Order*, 119–20; topicalization and focusing account for 56.6% of the clauses that Moshavi examines. Those cases of fronting which do not fall into the categories of topicalization or focusing are called the residue. These either serving a discourse function (11.2%), a result of a fixed order expression (1.5%), or unexplained (30.6%).

[49] Moshavi, *Word Order*, 101.

[50] Ibid., 102.

or larger units of text (e.g., because, so, but, etc.). However, the exact
nature of the relationship is often left to the reader to infer. Moshavi
illustrates this with the various possible relationships that English 'so'
can communicate.

> (1) I was sick, so I didn't come to school.
> (2) He missed school, so he must have been sick.

In example (1), "so" indicates that the second clause is a result of the
actions of the first clause. In example (2) "so" indicates the presence
of reasoning on the part of the speaker. The second clause is an inference made on the basis on the information in the first.

Moshavi argues that topicalization is a "kind of generalized
discourse connective."[51] Therefore, when an item is fronted for topicalization it signals that there is a coherence relation between the segment it occurs in and another segment and invites the readers to infer
the nature of the relationship. It is worth noting that the preposed constituent as a whole might not be the specific subject of topicalization.
Often the subject of the topicalization brings closely connected elements with it when it is fronted. For example, prepositions—often the
prepositional phrase as a whole will be fronted, but the subject of the
topicalization can be the object of the preposition and not the preposition itself. Furthermore, clauses with a fronted constituent can be
linked to the clause before it (backwards-linking; which is more common) or to the following clause (forward-linking).[52]

The actual relationships conveyed by topicalization vary. The
most common are the marking of opposition or similarity, with opposition being the most common overall.[53] An opposition relationship
highlights the difference between two constituents. A relationship of
similarity focuses on common ground. Moshavi notes that such relationships are communicated with English connectives such as 'like-

---

[51] Ibid., 103.
[52] Ibid., 101.
[53] Ibid., 155.

wise' or 'similarly.'[54] In the Sodom episode, Gen 18:33 serves as a good example of topicalization. Abraham is fronted to highlight the similarity between his departure and YHWH's.[55]

Gen 18:33 וַיֵּלֶךְ יְהוָה כַּאֲשֶׁר כִּלָּה לְדַבֵּר אֶל־אַבְרָהָם וְאַבְרָהָם שָׁב לִמְקֹמוֹ׃

4.2.2.2. Focusing

In Moshavi's treatment of focus, she adopts Jeanette Gundel's informational focus as the most useful definition. The focus is the "part of the proposition expressed by the sentence that is assumed by the speaker/writer to be new, rather than given."[56] Moshavi further interacts with the advancements of Lambrecht, who identified three different types of informational focus. Moshavi argues that Lambrecht's sentence and predicate focuses relate "entirely different" types of given information than does his argument focus. Therefore, the two should be separated. Moshavi's conception of informational focus is limited to Lambrecht's argument focus, which she renames constituent focus.[57]

By saying that focus is "part of the proposition...that is new rather than given" it is meant that focus identifies a particular constituent as a previously unknown part of an incomplete proposition in the mind of the reader/listener. Another way to state this is that the focus

---

[54] Ibid., 160; Lesser occurring coherence relationships are those which Moshavi classifies as speech-act relations. These include *addition, elaboration, summary,* and *paraphrase.* Moshavi provides few examples of these. Addition can be described as the speaker adding conditions or elements to something previously established—"In addition to X, Y will happen ...." Elaboration can be both backwards or forwards. In a forwards-linking elaboration a fronted constituent is further elaborated on in the following clause or clauses. In a backwards-linking clause the fronted constituent signals that its clause is the elaboration on a constituent in the previous clause, usually identifiable in some way with the fronted constituent. See Moshavi, *Word Order,* 161–63.

[55] Ibid., 161.

[56] Ibid., 90.

[57] Ibid., 90–91.

"[answers] an implicit wh-question."[58] This means that when a constituent is fronted for focus there is an incomplete proposition (such as "X went to the store") inferable or known from the previous context. The implicit wh-question form of this proposition would be "Who went to the store?" The focused element fills in the X/answers the question (i.e., *Bill* went to the store.")

בְּנֵי יַעֲקֹב בָּאוּ עַל־הַחֲלָלִים וַיָּבֹזּוּ הָעִיר אֲשֶׁר טִמְּאוּ אֲחוֹתָם: אֶת־צֹאנָם וְאֶת־בְּקָרָם וְאֶת־
חֲמֹרֵיהֶם וְאֵת אֲשֶׁר־בָּעִיר וְאֶת־אֲשֶׁר בַּשָּׂדֶה לָקָחוּ: Gen 34:27-28

In the example above, the object, "their sheep and their cattle..." is fronted as it answers the implicit question (What did they take?) raised by the earlier statement, "They plundered the city."[59]

Moshavi further elaborates on what it means for a proposition to be "given" in the above definition. Two types of given-ness are discussed—presupposed information and activated information. Presupposed information is common information shared by the speaker and the addressee. It is "part of [their] common ground."[60] The speaker can assume that it is known and believed by the addressee by virtue of their context, history, situation, etc. Activated information is what the speaker can assume is in the immediate consciousness of the addressee "at the time of the utterance."[61] The information is in the immediate consciousness because immediately preceding parts of the discourse would have put it there. Moshavi claims that activated is the relevant type of information when it comes to focusing in BH. She concludes based on her examination of Genesis that "[i]n narrative, focused clauses relate in every case to a proposition contained in or derived from the previous clause..."[62]

By saying "contained in *or* derived from" Moshavi means to highlight that an activated proposition does not need to be explicitly

---

[58] Ibid., 91.

[59] Ibid., 129.

[60] Ibid., 92–93.

[61] Ibid., 93

[62] Ibid., 97.

contained in the previous clause. When one reads a clause, they must interpret it using significant background knowledge and experience. Moshavi writes, "The mental representation incorporates inferences based on the reader's knowledge and experience; information not explicitly referred to in the text may nonetheless constitute activated information."[63]

Four types focusing are distinguished by Moshavi —identificational, substitutive, descriptive, and additive.[64] Each type refers to different ways the fronted constituent relates to the X factor of the proposition. Identificational is the most obvious and was used above in defining focusing. It refers to when the X is unknown and the focused constituent gives a value. The other types of focus involve the addressee already possessing a value for X in the proposition. Therefore, strictly speaking, not all types of focus involve answering a wh-question.[65]

Substitutive focusing occurs in contexts where a value is known or believed for X, but the speaker wishes to replace it with a different value. In this case, the focused constituent is meant to take the place of another constituent that is either implicitly or explicitly occupying the relevant role in a proposition. For example, the activated proposition is "X won the race" and the value the addressee has in mind is "Tom won the race." A substitutive focusing would be, "No, *Bill* won the race." In the Sodom episode, the fronted constituent "in the street" in 19:2 is fronted to contrast it with Lot's original offer to

---

[63] Ibid., 124.

[64] Ibid., 127–35; see Moshavi's work for many more Biblical examples of each. I will summarize their meanings and give an individual example borrowed from Moshavi.

[65] Ibid., 130; Moshavi herself recognizes this, but still chooses to define focus around the wh-question earlier in her book. In an older article, Moshavi provides a more general definition of focus that fits all the different types of focus. See Moshavi, "The Discourse Functions of Object/Adverbial-Fronting in Biblical Hebrew," in *Biblical Hebrew in Its Northwest Semitic Setting: Typological and Historical Perspectives*, ed. Steven E. Fassberg and Avi Hurvitz (Winona Lake, IN: Eisenbrauns, 2006), 235.

"stay in the house of your servant."

וַיֹּאמֶר הִנֶּה נָּא־אֲדֹנַי סוּרוּ נָא אֶל־בֵּית עַבְדְּכֶם וְלִינוּ וְרַחֲצוּ רַגְלֵיכֶם וְהִשְׁכַּמְתֶּם וַהֲלַכְתֶּם לְדַרְכְּכֶם וַיֹּאמְרוּ לֹּא כִּי בָרְחוֹב נָלִין: Gen 19:2

In descriptive focusing, a value for X is already held in the mind of the addressee and the speaker wishes to elaborate by giving a new value that is referentially identical. Such as the following:[66] "My wife really loves to swim (the activated proposition is X likes to swim). She always has a club membership and goes every chance she gets. She even takes our newborn with her. *Lexi* really loves to swim." This differs from substitutive in that the new "X" is not a replacement, but rather a new way of referring to X. In Gen 6:17 below, "all which is on the earth" is a restatement of the previously mentioned "all flesh which has the breath of life in it."

וַאֲנִי הִנְנִי מֵבִיא אֶת־הַמַּבּוּל מַיִם עַל־הָאָרֶץ לְשַׁחֵת כָּל־בָּשָׂר אֲשֶׁר־בּוֹ רוּחַ חַיִּים מִתַּחַת הַשָּׁמָיִם כֹּל אֲשֶׁר־בָּאָרֶץ יִגְוָע: Gen 6:17

Additive focusing also begins with the addressee having a value for X. However, instead of replacing that value (substitutive), or describing it by way of a new designation (descriptive), additive focusing does not negate X, but indicates that a new element should be added to X. In a situation where the proposition is "X likes to swim" and the current value for X that the addressee has is "Lexi likes to swim", an additive focus would be the statement, "*My kids* also like to swim." In Gen 35:12, "and to your offspring after you" is fronted to highlight that it is an addition to the promise "I will give the land to you."

וְאֶת־הָאָרֶץ אֲשֶׁר נָתַתִּי לְאַבְרָהָם וּלְיִצְחָק לְךָ אֶתְּנֶנָּה וּלְזַרְעֲךָ אַחֲרֶיךָ אֶתֵּן אֶת־הָאָרֶץ: Gen 35:12

---

[66] Understanding that the speaker's wife is named Lexi.

4.3. VSO–Aaron Hornkohl (2003)

Aaron Hornkohl wrote his MA thesis at the Hebrew University of Jerusalem on the pragmatics of the fronted constituents in clauses. He refers to clauses with fronted constituents as the X-V clauses, since he adopts a VSO view. The work is thorough for its size and well received. Holmstedt refers to it as "perhaps the best attempt [to situate VSO in a modern linguistic framework]."[67]

4.3.1. Hornkohl on Basic Word Order

Hornkohl provides four arguments for assuming a VSO order: statistical dominance, statistical dominance with preceding particles, the markedness of non-VSO word order with preceding function words, and descriptive simplicity.

Statistical dominance has been discussed thoroughly at this point and does not need rehashing. VSO is the statistically dominant word order. The reason for a specific tally of VSO orders with a preceding particle is to address the fact that *wayyiqtols* are variously interpreted.[68] Hornkohl avoids having to decide between competing interpretations and demonstrates that VSO is the dominant order even when consecutive clauses are excluded.

Hornkohl also applies the pragmatic criteria identified by Holmstedt. For Hornkohl this is "the most compelling and most complex for establishing basic word order."[69] Hornkohl's point in his initial argument is that most SV clauses in Genesis can be accounted for with a pragmatic interpretation and do not represent basic word order. Presumably, Hornkohl would argue that Holmstedt's identification of so many pragmatically marked SVO clauses in Ruth and Jonah as evidence against the basic correctness of Holmstedt's view

Finally, Hornkohl argues that a VSO order provides the greatest descriptive simplicity.[70] In cases where a constituent other than the

---

[67] Holmstedt, "Typological Classification of Word Order," 4n7.
[68] Hornkohl, "Pragmatics of the X-Verb Structure," 14.
[69] Ibid., 11.
[70] Ibid., 18–19.

verb or subject is fronted, the resultant order is overwhelmingly XVS. This structure can be explained by a one-step process from a VSO point of view. However from an SVO point of view, a two-step process must be adopted. First the X constituent must be fronted (transformation 1) and then the verb must be fronted ahead of the subject (transformation 2). Therefore it is simpler to explain XVS order from a VSO point of view. Hornkohl critiques Holmstedt's explanation of XVS clauses with triggered inversion as pragmatically unmotivated and inadequate.[71]

4.3.2. Hornkohl's Information Structure

Hornkohl's account of X-Verb clauses is that they convey one of two possible categories of pragmatic functions—focal and non-focal. Non-focal functions can be further divided into cases where the fronted constituent itself is what is being marked and when the clause as a whole is being marked by the fronting of a constituent. Many have recognized the stark difference between these two different types of fronting. At times, some have tried to understand all cases of fronting under only one of the frameworks (describing all fronted constituents as "emphatic"). However, most have come to admit that it is necessary to speak of multiple functions of fronting. One of the primary purposes of Hornkohl's work is to try and provide a unifying understanding of these two very different types of functions.

4.3.2.1. Focal Frontings

For Hornkohl, one of the purposes of fronting is to mark the fronted constituent as the focus of the clause. Focus is defined by Hornkohl as "the surface-level clausal element (rather than its informational referent) that is specially marked by the X+verb word order as bearing the most important or salient information in the clause."[72] The focus is marked by definition. Not every clause has a focus in Hornkohl's definitions, but only clauses where the most salient piece

---

[71] Ibid., 19–20.
[72] Ibid., 35.

of information is not the syntactic predicate. As Hornkohl observes, this means that, "the category of focal elements is limited to syntactic subjects and pieces of the syntactic predicate (be they complements or adjuncts)."[73] Therefore, Hornkohl does not use the term focus in relationship to an unmarked clause. There is no such thing as an unmarked focus for Hornkohl.

Hornkohl categorizes all occurrences of focus in Genesis under the following headings: focus for contrast, focus for fill-in/completion/identification, focus for contraexpected information, and focus for general reinforcement.[74] Focus of contrast and focus for identification overlap with the categories identified by Moshavi and others. For the purpose of saving space, I will not elaborate further. However, Hornkohl is somewhat unique in distinguishing between a focus for contrast and a topicalization for contrast. Focus of contraexpected information Hornkohl describes as a "subtype" of focus for contrast.[75] In such cases, the fronted constituent is not being contrasted with a specific constituent in the preceding or following context, but rather with a general expectation. The fronted constituent is a surprise relative to the general expectation. Hornkohl does not define focus for general reinforcement beyond its title.[76]

---

[73] Ibid., 36.

[74] Ibid., 38–40.

[75] Ibid., 40.

[76] Instead, Hornkohl reserves his discussion under the "General Reinforcement" heading to a defense of the subjective nature of identifying such focusing as general reinforcement. His point is a helpful reminder for those who wish linguistic investigation would be as rigid as the hard sciences; "For some scholars, the lack of an objectively verifiable definition constitutes grounds for exclusion of such examples from consideration. However, many language 'rules' are optional, employed by speakers and writers subjectively. If a full linguistic account of a language must relate to these optional rules—and it is taken as an axiom here that this is, indeed, the case—then it must allow for form-function-meaning relationships that defy unambiguous definition" ("Pragmatics of the X-Verb Structure," 40).

4.3.2.2. Non-Focal Frontings

Hornkohl points out that fronting for focus represents only the minority of cases of fronting in Genesis. Far more often the fronted constituent is serving one of two general non-focal functions. The first type of non-focal functions can be described as those cases where the constituent fronted is itself the item being marked. Hornkohl is content to use the language of topic and topicalization for this phenomenon. According to Hornkohl's definitions, in BH a constituent can be fronted "[i]n order to mark it as the subject matter for what follows, be it a paragraph or a one-line statement."[77] This can manifest itself in a number of specific applications in practice. A constituent can be fronted for the purpose of introducing a new topic. A constituent that is not truly the topic of the larger discourse can be topicalized and made a "temporary topic" in order to comment on it. Finally, an already active constituent might be topicalized in order to contrast it with something else.

Hornkohl delineates between contrastive topicalization and contrastive focus.[78] When a constituent is topicalized for contrast, the point of contrast is something about the constituent (an action or attribute) and not the constituent itself. A subject which is topicalized for contrast is having its actions compared with another actor in the discourse (i.e., "*Tom* went home, but *Bill* stayed.") The contrast in is in the two different actions by Tom and Bill. Whereas a constituent that is fronted for contrastive focus is itself the point of contrast. E.g., "I like *apples*, not pears."

Following in the footsteps of many others, Hornkohl recognizes a problem with the association of all types of non-focal fronting as marking a topic. The most obvious problem is the existence of clauses where it seems to be the clause as a whole that is marked by the fronting of an individual constituent. Some studies, such as Moshavi's, have left these to the side and focused on the pragmatics of when particular constituents are marked. Others have focused on the marked

---

[77] Ibid., 47.

[78] Ibid., 38.

clauses. Still others have sought for some sort of unifying principle that could accurately described both types of marking.[79] Hornkohl is similar to Buth in seeking an overarching description for both types of non-focal fronting. He accomplishes this with the idea of discourse continuity.

A discourse is a series of clauses/sentences that form a coherent whole. Hornkohl says that a discourse "exhibits pragmatic continuity by definition."[80] Written work, as with any medium, is limited in how it can portray events. Events that were simultaneous in reality cannot be simultaneously related. There must be some sort of sequencing in written work. This is why narrative sequence often, but not always, corresponds to temporal sequence. Because a narrative as a discourse must have continuity, this also means "in narrative, there quite naturally exists a high correlation between continuity and sequentiality" without there being an exact identity between the two.[81]

With regard to BH, Hornkohl posits that the *wayyiqtol* form is used to mark continuity. It is a pragmatic way to "establish and preserve" continuity in a discourse. The problems with trying to identify the *wayyiqtol* with sequentiality are solved. The *wayyiqtol* will often represent a sequence in narrative, because of the strong overlap between narrative continuity and sequentiality, but it is not obligated to portray sequence in narrative.[82]

Returning to the issue of non-focal fronting, Hornkohl posits that all such occurrences can be understood as interrupting the pragmatic concept of continuity. Non-focal fronting communicates discourse discontinuity. This means that X-Verb structures that are not

---

[79] Stephen H. Levinsohn, "Unmarked and Marked Instances of Topicalization in Hebrew," in *Work papers of the Summer Institute of Linguistics,* ed. Robert A. Dooley and John Clifton (Dallas: SIL, 1990), 21–33; also Buth, "Functional Grammar," 84–93.

[80] Hornkohl's "pragmatic continuity" is synonymous with the concept of coherence.

[81] Hornkohl, "Pragmatics of the X-Verb Structure," 61.

[82] Ibid., 62; Hornkohl hypothesizes that the same might be true of *weqatal* and non-narrative material. However, he does not focus on such in his study.

focusing or topicalizing are not necessarily interrupting a temporal sequence, though they certainly may be.

The idea of discourse discontinuity unifies the two types of non-focal fronting. Both a marked constituent or a marked clause can be subsumed under the general heading of discontinuity. One can interrupt continuity to mark a particular constituent as a topic or one can interrupt continuity to mark an entire clause as non-sequential, or any other number of functions that can be described as pragmatically discontinuous.[83]

4.4. Excursus: Outlier Positions

It almost seems too obvious to point out, but there are more than two positions in this debate. That is, there are more than the SVO and VSO camps.[84] There are also positions that argue against a basic word order as defined in the previous two chapters altogether.[85] For the sake of completeness, I have included a brief survey of two recent works that represent some of these "outlier" positions.

4.4.1. Katsuomi Shimasaki (2002)

Katsuomi Shimasaki's dissertation was expanded and published as *Focus Structure in Biblical Hebrew*. His work is rooted in the

---

[83] Therefore, Hornkohl's idea of pragmatic discontinuity covers the concept of topic marking, as well as clauses that have been elsewhere described as background information, offline comments, starting new units, etc.

[84] This recognition is apart from the even more basic recognition that neither the VSO or SVO camp is a monolith. The specific pragmatic proposals of various proponents as well as the understanding of what "basic word order" means sometimes differs widely even within camps as we have seen in the survey above.

[85] These various positions seem to be unified in seeing the first position of the clause as having a special, psychological significance. E. J. Revell, "The Conditioning of Word Order in Verbless Clauses in Biblical Hebrew," *JSS* 34.1 (1989): 1–24; "System," 1–37; and "Thematic Continuity and the Conditioning of Word Order in Verbless Clauses," in *The Verbless Clause in Biblical Hebrew: Linguistic Approaches*, ed. Cynthia L. Miller (Winona Lake, IN: Eisenbrauns, 1999), 297–320. According to Revell, authors order the constituents in their sentence by descending importance ("System," 21).

work of Knud Lambrecht. Shimasaki's work provides a unified analysis for both verbal and nominal clauses. There are not disparate word orders between them, but rather, Shimasaki views the clause initial position as fundamentally marked for focus. This is regardless of clause type. To focus an item is to "mark it as informationally prominent."[86]

Shimasaki's focus structure is built upon an argument-predicate binary. He follows Lambrecht in defining an argument as a discourse referent and a predicate as an attribute of, or relation between arguments.[87] The argument is more broadly defined than subject and can include the syntactical subject, object, etc. The most salient question for Shimasaki is whether an argument or the predicate of a clause is occupying the focused position (the first position). The answer to this question determines the pragmatic function of the clause.

Following Lambrecht, Shimasaki identifies three possible focus structures: predicate focus, argument focus, and clause focus.[88] Predicate focus is signaled by a predicate-argument order. Argument focus is signaled by an argument-predicate order. Clause focus has an identical structure to argument focus (argument-predicate) but Shimasaki hypothesizes that it would have also included a vocal pitch

---

[86] Katsuomi Shimasaki, *Focus Structure in Biblical Hebrew* (Bethesda, MD: CDL, 2002), 42.

[87] Ibid., 44. Shimasaki provides this full quote from Knud Lambrecht, *Information Structure and Sentence Form: Topic, Focus, and the Mental Representations of Discourse Referents* (Cambridge: Cambridge University Press, 1994), 75; "Discourse referents are syntactically expressed in ARGUMENT (including adjunct) categories, such as noun phrases, pronouns, various kinds of tensed or non-tensed subordinate clauses, and certain adverbial phrases (those that can be said to refer to the circumstances of a predication). They cannot normally be expressed in phrases that serve as PREDICATES. Predicates by definition do not denote discourse referents but attributes of, or relations between, arguments. For example a finite verb phrase cannot play an argument role in a sentence unless it is made into a referential expression by being "nominalized."

[88] Lambrecht originally used the term "sentence focus" for what Shimasaki calls the "clause focus." Lambrecht, *Informaton Structure*, 221–35; here can be found his original discussion of the three focuses.

stress that would have differentiated between the two.[89]

Predicate-focus communicates that the clause is adding new information to an already known referent/topic.[90] Shimasaki calls this "commenting."

> (1) Tom skipped breakfast.
> (2) He is *hungry*.

In (2) the predicate is focused by pitch. The point is to comment on the already active topic Tom (represented with a pronoun).

Argument focus is described as "identificational."[91] It is used to indicate that the fronted argument is supplying the missing argument of an incomplete proposition. This can be illustrated with a question-answer example.

> (3) Who is hungry?
> (4) *Tom* is hungry.

In the above exchange, Tom (an argument) is focused by pitch. Clause (4) is identifying X in the proposition "X is hungry." The point of (4) is not to comment on Tom.

Finally, there is clause focus. It is identified by a double focus.

> (5) *Tom* became *hungry*.

This category functions as a catch-all and is used whenever commenting or identifying is not the purpose of the clause in question. Functions that a clause focus structure might accomplish include: event reporting, presentations, exclamations, surprise, contrasting the whole proposition, presenting topic of a new episode, starting a new episode.[92]

---

[89] Shimasaki, *Focus Structure*, 57–58.
[90] Ibid., 50–51.
[91] Ibid., 51.
[92] Ibid., 51–52; Shimasaki defines clause-focus more broadly than Lam-

It can be seen in this brief survey that it would not be proper to classify Shimasaki in the VSO camp. In fact, Shimasaki addresses the idea of VSO being the unmarked order and argues against it.[93] In the information structure presented here, all word orders are marked for specific pragmatic functions.

4.4.2. Kyoungwon Choi (2006)

Kyoungwon Choi did his dissertation on SV clauses in Genesis at SBTS under Dr. Russell Fuller.[94] Choi maintains the traditional Arabic grammarian definitions of nominal and verbal clauses.[95] This

---

brecht. For Lambrecht, clause-focus was not a catchall and was only used for functions such as event reporting and exclamations (*Information Structure*, 140).

[93] Ibid., 114–21. I would argue that Robert Holmstedt's critique of Shimasaki for assuming VS to be the normal sequence misses the mark a bit. Shimasaki makes it clear as the volume progresses that VS order is only normal in that Predicate-Focus is the most commonly used focus in narrative discourse. Nonetheless, Robert Holmstedt's review is quite helpful; "Adjusting Our Focus (Review of Katsuomi Shimasaki, *Focus Structure in Biblical Hebrew: A Study of Word Order and Information Structure*)," *Hebrew Studies* 44 (2003): 203–15.

[94] The dissertation has been published unchanged; Choi, *An Analysis of Subject-Before-Finite-Verb Clauses in the Book of Genesis Based on Traditional Grammarians* (Saarbrücken: VDM Verlag Dr. Müller, 2008).

[95] See Choi, *Analysis*, 1–5. See Chapter 5 in his work for his defense of the traditional view (101–12). Alviero Niccacci also maintains the Arabian definitions in his work, *The Syntax of the Verb in Classical Hebrew* (Sheffield: Sheffield Academic, 1990), 23-28 and 166-67. After an examination of the data, Niccacci concludes that the normal word order for the narrative verbal clause as well as speech (which Niccacci calls 'discourse') is VS (174–75). I am not certain what it means to say that the "normal" order for a verbal clause is VS, if an SV word order always represents a different clause type. This same distinction is maintained in another recent dissertation done under Russell Fuller—Richard Charles Macdonald, "Grammatical Analysis of Various Biblical Hebrew Texts According to a Traditional Semitic Grammar" (PhD diss., Southern Baptist Theological Seminary, 2014). Macdonald differs from Niccacci in holding that a fronted adverb or object would not change the verbal nature of the clause ("Grammatical Analysis," 137). The predominance of VS order is attributed to the semantic value of verbal clauses being uniquely suited for carrying a narrative, Macdonald, "Grammatical Analysis," 138. Macdonald's dissertation relies heavily on the then unreleased Hebrew syntax textbook by Fuller and Choi, *Biblical*

definition is based on the type of word that occupies the first position in a clause. A clause that has a finite verb in the first position is a verbal clause. Conversely, when a clause has a noun in the first position it is a nominal clause. If a nominal clause has a finite verb in the predicate then it is considered a compound nominal clause (CNC). A verbal clause, by definition, must begin with the verb.

Choi still holds that BH should be classified as a VSO language (he calls VS the "normal" order), but in many ways, his analysis should be thought of as a type of free-order analysis. His understanding of "basic" word order in the literature is flawed and the insistence on VSO as normal creates equivocation.[96] Following traditional Arabic grammar, clauses with a noun preceding the verb are not verbal clauses with a fronted constituent. Such clauses are viewed as a different type of clause, the CNC, with a different function. In this sense, all word orders are "marked" and there is no basic word order from which the others are produced by any transformation. Nor is there any direct placing of a constituent in a position that it does not normally occupy.[97]

It is worth mentioning that Choi features a unique argument for his conception of VSO, that I have not encountered elsewhere in the literature. Choi points out the Masoretic accent tradition supports his analysis. When the word order is VS, the Masoretes usually link the

---

Hebrew Syntax: A Traditional Semitic Approach (Grand Rapids: Kregel, forthcoming). It has since been released as *An Invitation to Biblical Hebrew Syntax: An Intermediate Grammar* (Grand Rapids: Kregel, 2017). Presumably, this work will serve as a modern standard for the traditional Arabic grammarian distinction.

[96] Unfortunately for his analysis, Choi does not understand what Holmstedt and others have meant by "pragmatically neutral." He supposes that this might mean "dispassionate" or spoken "in a calm state of mind." See Choi, *Analysis*, 107.

[97] Space precludes a detailed examination of the views represented by Niccacci, Fuller, Choi, and Macdonald. For an argument against the CNC (and the Arabic grammarian definitions of nominal and verbal clauses) there is Walter Gross, "Is There Really a Compound Nominal Clause in Biblical Hebrew?" in *The Verbless Clause in Biblical Hebrew: Linguistic Approaches*, ed. Cynthia L. Miller (Winona Lake, IN: Eisenbrauns, 1999), 297–320.

verb to the following subject with a conjunctive accent. However, when the order is SV, the Masoretes usually separate the two, placing a disjunctive accent on the initial subject.[98]

4.5. Some Summarizing Thoughts on the Word Order and Pragmatics Debate

When the issue is pressed and the authors are compared, I argue that the question of basic word order and pragmatic markedness can be narrowed down to a lowest common denominator—simple SV and VS clauses with no other constituent fronted.[99] Such clauses are at the heart of the debate and allow common ground discussion.

There is debate on the place of the consecutive forms. There is debate over the proper theoretical linguistic framework to approach the issue. There are challenges to Holmstedt's appeal to triggered inversion to account for most VS clauses. And so on and so forth. However, if these questions are bracketed there is still a way to adjudicate the debate, and that is by assessing the pragmatic status of the first constituent in simple indicative SV and VS clauses with no other fronted constituent.

In Holmstedt's SV information structure system, SV clauses can be either basic or marked. However, all simple indicative VS orders "without a syntactic or semantic trigger" must be considered to have the verb pragmatically marked for either topic or focus.[100]

In both Moshavi and Hornkohl's information structure system, all SV orders must be considered to have either the subject marked or the clause marked (for discourse structure or pragmatic reasons).[101] Both Moshavi and Hornkohl would not describe a VS order to have a pragmatically marked verb, but theoretically, a similar strategy to Holmstedt's could account for VS clauses with pragmatically marked

---

[98] Choi, *Analysis*, 110.

[99] By 'simple' I mean clauses that do not employ "consecutive" forms. So only *qatal* or *yiqtol* clauses are considered.

[100] Holmstedt, "Word Order and Information Structure," 138.

[101] Moshavi's work does contain a residue of unexplained fronted clauses.

verbs in a VS system. Therefore, the key question between the two views from the pragmatic side is: which view most convincingly accounts for simple clauses of word orders that depart from their proposed basic word order? For an SV system, it is the status of verbs in VS clauses that is most salient. For a VS system, it is the status of subjects in SV clauses.

4.6. Applying the Views to the Sodom Episode (Gen 18-19)

The purpose of this book is not to decide between the two positions. The goal is to determine the practical difference between the two in reading. One step towards answering questions of difference has already been made in identifying the most salient clause type in the debate. The next step is to illustrate the difference by applying the views to a discourse. In the two commentaries on the Sodom episode in the following chapters, first a VSO system and then an SVO system will be applied. Each commentary will assume the correctness of the basic word order and accompanying information structure and apply them rigidly. The point of the commentaries is not to evaluate the proposed view, but to test what types of reading it produces so that these can be compared with the alternate viewpoint.

4.7. Excursus: Introduction to The Sodom Episode

In order to give context to any exegetical ramifications of the data produced in the word order commentaries, I would like to briefly introduce the content and themes of Gen 18–19. The book of Genesis is concerned with God's covenant promise to Abraham and his family and the outworking of these promises in history. The first eleven chapters of Genesis focus on primordial history and all of mankind. The rest of the book narrows to dealing with Abraham and his offspring.

There is a reason the book starts with the creation of all things, moves to mankind in general, and ends focusing on one family. The claim of the book of Genesis is that there is a unique role that Abraham and his offspring are playing in the entire history of the cosmos.

The first eleven chapters are inextricably linked to the following thirty-nine chapters. This is true on both a literary and theological level.

At the point in the narrative when the Sodom episode begins, the author has already introduced God's call on Abraham and His threefold promise of land, seed, and blessing (12:1–2). Abraham leaves Ur with Sarah and Lot and makes his way to the land of Canaan. In Gen 17, God promises that Abraham will have a biological son with Sarah (17:15–17). This promise also includes the fact that the child born to Sarah will be the one YHWH establishes His covenant with (17:19).

Genesis 18–19 recounts a physical visit of YHWH to Abraham in the form of a man with two attendants,[102] the reaffirmation of the promise of a son to Sarah, the intercession of Abraham for Sodom, the angelic messengers' visit to Lot in Sodom, the destruction of Sodom, and the incestuous aftermath between Lot and his daughters. Numerous themes that are developed in the whole of Genesis and the wider Pentateuch are present in the Sodom episode: God's faithfulness and His ability to keep His word, judgment on the wicked,[103] righteousness, the importance of seed, intercession on behalf of sinners, and salvation.

In Gen 18 YHWH restates the promise of offspring to Abraham; a promise whose stated fulfillment will take a miracle (18:10–11). Furthermore, on the basis of His plan for Abraham, YHWH privately shares His plans to destroy Sodom (18:16–21). This prompts Abraham to intercede on behalf of any righteous people that may be present in Sodom (18:22–33). The wider theme of God's faithfulness to Abraham controls even Gen 19, where Abraham is mostly absent as a character. Abraham's intercession for Sodom is meant to stay prominent in the reader's mind throughout Gen 19, and God's salvation of

---

[102] Victor P. Hamilton, *The Book of Genesis: Chapters 18–50* (Grand Rapids: Eerdmans, 1995), 7–8.

[103] Gordon J. Wenham, *Genesis 26–50*, WBC 2 (Waco, TX: Word, 1994), 41–45. Wenham elaborates on a number of parallels between the Sodom episode and Noah's flood episode (Gen 6–9).

Lot and his family from the destruction is summarized as God re-membering Abraham (19:29). Numerous elements in the narrative it-self point to a comparison between Lot and Abraham:[104] their parallel starting positions, greetings, the act of food preparation, their response to the judgment of Sodom, etc.[105] The positive portrayal of Abraham coupled with the negative elements of Lot's character, further suggests that it is on account of Abraham's righteousness that Lot is spared.[106]

---

[104] David W. Cotter, *Genesis in Berit Olam: Studies in Hebrew Narrative & Poetry* (Collegeville, MN: Liturgical Press, 2003), 117.

[105] Wenham, *Genesis 26–50*, 43–44.

[106] Cotter, *Genesis*, 127–28.

Chapter 5
GENESIS 18–19: A VSO COMMENTARY

This chapter will present a graphically laid out syntactic outline of Gen 18–19 with word order relevant labels and commentary. The commentary will assume a VSO point of view and discuss the information structures of Moshavi and Hornkohl. Given that VSO is the majority position, I will also occasionally interact with any commentaries on Genesis that make word order observations.[1]

5.1. On the Hebrew Text Layout
For the Hebrew text itself, each clause is given a separate line, with two exceptions: (1) when clauses function as constituents within another clause (i.e. as the object/complement of a verb); and (2) in the case of verbal hendiadys the two verbs are left on the same line in order to save space. Clauses that are syntactically subordinate to the previous clause are indented. Relative clauses, though syntactically imbedded in another clause are also given a separate line for the purpose of ease of visual representation. They are indented to begin underneath their heads. Direct speech is in gray font.

5.2. Word Order Labels
The main three constituents of S, V, and O are in **boldface** for easy identification. Compound subjects and objects are treated as a single constituent and labeled S or O respectively. The appearance of a double object (O-O) indicates a double accusative construction, which could theoretically be rendered with one object and an indirect object (e.g., "I taught him the piano" vs "I taught the piano to him").

---

[1] All translations in the commentary section are my own, unless otherwise noted.

Many constituents are composed of more than one word. For long complex constituents, I have elaborated on their individual make-ups. These specifications immediately follow the constituent in parentheses; i.e., TempP (Prep-Inf-S-O).

Oblique objects (objects marked by prepositions) are marked as O and not PP. Indirect objects are marked as IO and not PP. Locations marked with the locative ה are considered adverbial accusatives. Clauses that are considered marked are underlined on the labeling.[2]

5.3. Sodom Commentary: VSO

18:1a וַיֵּרָא אֵלָיו יְהוָה בְּאֵלֹנֵי מַמְרֵא
1b וְהוּא יֹשֵׁב פֶּתַח־הָאֹהֶל כְּחֹם הַיּוֹם:

18:1a   V-IO-S-PP
1b   S-V(Ptcpl)-AA-PP

2a וַיִּשָּׂא עֵינָיו
2b וַיַּרְא
2c וְהִנֵּה שְׁלֹשָׁה אֲנָשִׁים נִצָּבִים עָלָיו

2a   **V-O**
2b   **V**
2c   Part-**S-V**(Ptcpl)-PP

2d וַיַּרְא וַיָּרָץ לִקְרָאתָם מִפֶּתַח הָאֹהֶל
2e וַיִּשְׁתַּחוּ אָרְצָה:

2d   **V-V-Comp-PP**
2e   **V-AA**

3a וַיֹּאמַר
3b אֲדֹנָי אִם־נָא מָצָאתִי חֵן בְּעֵינֶיךָ
3c   אַל־נָא תַעֲבֹר מֵעַל עַבְדֶּךָ:

---

[2] That is, marked by fronting a constituent before the verb. Post-verbal movement, left-dislocation, and right-dislocation, as well as other forms of marking will not be treated in this commentary.

3a   **V**
3b   Voc-**V**-**O**-PP
3c   **V**-PP

יְקַּֽח־נָ֣א מְעַט־מַ֫יִם 4a
וְרַחֲצ֖וּ רַגְלֵיכֶ֑ם 4b
וְהִֽשָּׁעֲנ֖וּ תַּ֥חַת הָעֵֽץ׃ 4c

4a   **V**-S
4b   **V**-O
4c   **V**-PP

וְאֶקְחָ֨ה פַת־לֶ֜חֶם 5a
וְסַעֲד֣וּ לִבְּכֶ֗ם 5b
אַחַ֣ר תַּעֲבֹ֔רוּ 5c
כִּֽי־עַל־כֵּ֥ן עֲבַרְתֶּ֖ם עַֽל־עַבְדְּכֶ֑ם 5d

5a   **V**-O
5b   **V**-S
5c   PP-**V**
5d   Part(Part-PP)-**V**-O

וַיֹּ֣אמְר֔וּ 5e
כֵּ֥ן תַּעֲשֶׂ֖ה 5f
כַּאֲשֶׁ֥ר דִּבַּֽרְתָּ׃ 5g

5e   **V**
5f   Part-**V**
5g   Rel-**V**

וַיְמַהֵ֧ר אַבְרָהָ֛ם הָאֹ֖הֱלָה אֶל־שָׂרָ֑ה 6a
וַיֹּ֕אמֶר 6b

6a   **V**-S-AA-PP
6b   **V**

מַהֲרִ֞י שְׁלֹ֤שׁ סְאִים֙ קֶ֣מַח סֹ֔לֶת 6c
ל֖וּשִׁי וַעֲשִׂ֥י עֻגֽוֹת׃ 6d

6c   **V**-O
6d   **V**-**V**-O

וְאֶל־הַבָּקָר רָץ אַבְרָהָם 7a
וַיִּקַּח בֶּן־בָּקָר רַךְ וָטוֹב 7b
וַיִּתֵּן אֶל־הַנַּעַר 7c
וַיְמַהֵר לַעֲשׂוֹת אֹתוֹ׃ 7d

7a   PP-V-S
7b   V-O
7c   V-PP
7d   V-Comp

The only fronted element is the prepositional phrase. The rest of the word order is standard. Wenham mentions the fronted order (indicating that it forms a chiasm with the previous action of Abraham in v. 6a) but does not elaborate on any meaning it may have.[3] Speiser indicates only that the order has been "inverted for special emphasis."[4]

Moshavi considers v. 7a to be an example of a clause with a fronted constituent that is sequential in the story.[5] The actors of the story have been Abraham and the three visitors up to this point. Verses 5 and 6 have focused on Abraham's preparations, with Abraham as the main actor. Abraham's two actions in preparation for the visitors—having Sarah make the flour cakes and having his servant prepare the meat—seem to be equally important and are naturally understood as temporally sequential. The fact that v. 7a begins without a *wayyiqtol* does not remove this clause from the main storyline.

Hornkohl also concludes that the actions are most likely reported chronologically. Due to the presence of the fronted constituent, Hornkohl argues that there must be some discontinuity going on.[6] Hornkohl suggests in the same section that the discontinuity in this case is "very general in nature" and might serve to slow down the action of the narrative.

Moshavi classifies v. 7a as one of seven ambiguous cases, where it can be argued that it could be either an example of topicaliza-

---

[3] Wenham, *Genesis 26–50*, 36.

[4] E. A. Speiser, *Genesis*, AB 1 (Garden City, NY: Doubleday, 1964), 130.

[5] Moshavi, *Word Order*, 31.

[6] Hornkohl, "Pragmatics of the X-Verb Structure," 64–65.

tion or focusing.[7] If the clause is topicalizing it can be assumed that it is either a relationship of contrast or similarity being conveyed. In which case the relationship would be between Abraham's actions and the presumed actions of Sarah following Abraham's instructions in vv. 6c-d.

Alternatively, the clause can be a focusing clause of addition.[8] The mention of the cattle is a surprise at this point. This is the first time anything is said of cattle. Abraham had only mentioned "a bite of bread" to the three visitors, nor had he said anything to Sarah. The proposition in mind is the previously stated "Abraham hurried to Sarah." Now "to the cattle" is focused in order to highlight that it is added and not part of the expected itinerary (i.e., "*Additionally*, Abraham ran *to the cattle*.")

8a וַיִּקַּח חֶמְאָ֨ה וְחָלָ֜ב וּבֶן־הַבָּקָר֙

8b אֲשֶׁ֣ר עָשָׂ֔ה

8c וַיִּתֵּ֖ן לִפְנֵיהֶ֑ם

8a	**V-O**
8b	Rel-V
8c	**V-PP**

8d וְהֽוּא־עֹמֵ֧ד עֲלֵיהֶ֛ם תַּ֥חַת הָעֵ֖ץ

8e וַיֹּאכֵֽלוּ׃

8d	**S-V(Ptcpl)-PP-PP**[9]
8e	**V**

9a וַיֹּאמְר֣וּ אֵלָ֔יו

9b אַיֵּ֖ה שָׂרָ֣ה אִשְׁתֶּ֑ךָ

9a	**V-PP**
9b	Q-**S**-(S-App)

---

[7] Moshavi, *Word Order*, 105.

[8] Ibid., 133–35.

[9] Subject-Participle is considered the basic word order in the VSO view as participles are treated as a type of nominal clause.

9c וַיֹּאמֶר

9d הִנֵּה בָאֹהֶל:

9c V
9d Part-PP

10a וַיֹּאמֶר

10b שׁוֹב אָשׁוּב אֵלֶיךָ כָּעֵת חַיָּה

10c וְהִנֵּה־בֵן לְשָׂרָה אִשְׁתֶּךָ

10a V
10b V-PP-PP
10c Part-**S-Pred** (PP-App)

10d וְשָׂרָה שֹׁמַעַת פֶּתַח הָאֹהֶל

10e וְהוּא אַחֲרָיו:

10d **S-V**(ptcpl)-AA
10e **S-Pred**(PP)

11a וְאַבְרָהָם וְשָׂרָה זְקֵנִים

11b בָּאִים בַּיָּמִים

11c חָדַל לִהְיוֹת לְשָׂרָה אֹרַח כַּנָּשִׁים:

11a **S-Pred**
11b **V**(Ptcpl)-PP
11c **V-PP-S**

12a וַתִּצְחַק שָׂרָה בְּקִרְבָּהּ לֵאמֹר

12b אַחֲרֵי בְלֹתִי הָיְתָה־לִּי עֶדְנָה

12c וַאדֹנִי זָקֵן:

12a **V-S-PP**
12b TempP[Prep-V(Inf)]-**V-PP-S**
12c <u>**S-V**</u>

The form זָקֵן could be either a 3MS *qatal* or an adjective. If it is a *qatal,* it is probably serving the same function as the S-V clause in v. 13d. Wenham considers both of these "circumstantial clauses turning a question into virtual negation."[10]

---

[10] Wenham, *Genesis 26–50*, 37, following Francis Andersen, *The Sentence*

13a וַיֹּאמֶר יְהוָה אֶל־אַבְרָהָם
13b לָמָּה זֶּה צָחֲקָה שָׂרָה לֵאמֹר
13c הַאַף אֻמְנָם אֵלֵד
13d וַאֲנִי זָקַנְתִּי׃

13a **V-S-IO**
13b Q-V-**S**
13c Q-Part-**V**
13d **S-V**

The S-V clause in v. 13d falls under the category of those which contain fronting not for the purpose of topicalization or focusing. Moshavi calls these clauses the residue. In Moshavi's discussions of the residue of subject fronted clauses, she notes that in the majority of cases, the purpose of the fronting is not to mark the fronted constituent, but the clause as a whole.[11] She concludes that clauses are marked by fronting subjects and not other constituents.

Hornkohl is content to understand the S-V clauses in v. 12c and v. 13d as conveying "circumstantial" information, according to Muraoka's definition of circumstantial.[12] Moshavi rejects the circumstantial interpretation.[13] In this instance Moshavi identifies the purpose of the clause as justification.[14] She observes a number of instances where a fronted clause follows a rhetorical question or command. In such environments, the fronted clause gives the reason for the command or question. Rhetorical questions often imply a negative proposition. Who could possibly eat that whole thing? Proposition: No one could eat the whole thing. A clause of justification gives the reasoning for holding to the implied proposition of a rhetorical question.

The rhetorical question in v. 13c can be translated "Shall I really bear (a child)?" implying the negative "I will surely not bear a

---

in Biblical Hebrew (The Hague: Mouton, 1974), 90.

[11] Moshavi, *Word Order*, 112; she identifies 75% of the residue of subject preposed clauses as marking the clause as a whole.

[12] Hornkohl, "Pragmatics of the X-Verb Structure," 67.

[13] Moshavi, *Word Order*, 20–21.

[14] Ibid., 116.

child." The fronted subject pronoun in v. 13d marks the entire clause as giving the reason for Sarah's belief in v. 13c. "I will not bear a child *because* I am old."

הֲיִפָּלֵא מֵיְהוָה דָּבָר 14a

לַמּוֹעֵד אָשׁוּב אֵלֶיךָ כָּעֵת חַיָּה 14b

וּלְשָׂרָה בֵן׃ 14c

14a   Q-V-PP-S
14b   PP-V-PP-PP
14c   **Pred(PP)-S**

Verse 14b is best understood as a case of descriptive focusing.[15] YHWH is reinforcing his ability to do what He promised. He has already indicated that He will return at "the time of life." "I will return at X and you will have a son" is active in Sarah's mind, as it is the very point in dispute. The "time of life" is further described as "the appointed time."

Verse 14c represents a special case of substitutional focus. In many cases of substitutional focus, the original value for X in the activated proposition is recently negated.[16] The proposition is "X will have a son" and the original value for X was Sarah. God had told Abraham in v. 10c that "Sarah will have a son" using an unmarked order for this first pronouncement. This has remained an active proposition. The following verses focused on Sarah's incredulity. Her rhetorical question in v. 12b functionally served as a negation, "No, I will not have a son." However, here YHWH does not replace the X with a different value, but fronts "to Sarah" in order to highlight that Sarah will in fact have a son. This despite however unlikely she may seem to be as a candidate to have a child when YHWH returns.

וַתְּכַחֵשׁ שָׂרָה לֵאמֹר 15a

לֹא צָחַקְתִּי 15b

כִּי יָרֵאָה 15c

---

[15] Ibid., 130–31.
[16] Ibid., 131–32.

15a   **V-S**
15b   **V**
15c   Part-**V**

15d וַיֹּאמֶר׀

15e לֹא כִּי צָחָקְתְּ׃

15d   **V**
15e   Neg-Part-**V**

16a וַיָּקֻמוּ מִשָּׁם הָאֲנָשִׁים
16b וַיַּשְׁקִפוּ עַל־פְּנֵי סְדֹם
16c וְאַבְרָהָם הֹלֵךְ עִמָּם
16d לְשַׁלְּחָם׃

16a   **V-PP-S**
16b   **V-PP**
16c   **S-V**(Ptcpl)-PP
16d   **V**

17a וַיהֹוָה אָמָר
17b הַמְכַסֶּה אֲנִי מֵאַבְרָהָם
17c אֲשֶׁר אֲנִי עֹשֶׂה׃

17a   <u>**S-V**</u>
17b   <u>Q-**V**(Ptcpl)-**S**-PP</u>
17c   Rel-**S-V**(Ptcpl)

Wenham describes vv. 17–19 as one complex circumstantial statement.[17] Moshavi and Hornkohl consider the subject fronting in v. 17a to be a case of the clause being marked as a whole to indicate the start of a new scene, characterized either by new participants or a new setting.[18] This clause is so identified either because YHWH becomes the speaker abruptly after the previous verse focused on the action of "the men" and "Abraham" or because the scene has shifted to the walk the men are on. The latter option is better in this case. YHWH had previously been a main speaker/actor in vv. 13–15.

---

[17] Wenham, *Genesis 26–50*, 37.

[18] Moshavi, *Word Order*, 115. Hornkohl, "Pragmatics of the X-Verb Structure," 69.

וְאַבְרָהָם הָיוֹ יִהְיֶה לְגוֹי גָּדוֹל וְעָצוּם 18a

וְנִבְרְכוּ בוֹ כָּל גּוֹיֵי הָאָרֶץ: 18b

18a   <u>S-V-Compl</u>
18b   **V-PP-S**

Moshavi classifies v. 18a as another instance of fronting not for topicalization or focus, but for clause marking. Verse 18a is a clause of justification. In the previous verse YHWH asks the rhetorical question, "Shall I hide from Abraham what I am doing?" The implied negative proposition is "I shall not hide what I am doing from Abraham." The subject is fronted here to indicate that this clause gives the reason why God will not hide anything from Abraham.

כִּי יְדַעְתִּיו 19a

לְמַעַן אֲשֶׁר יְצַוֶּה אֶת־בָּנָיו וְאֶת־בֵּיתוֹ אַחֲרָיו 19b

וְשָׁמְרוּ דֶּרֶךְ יְהוָה לַעֲשׂוֹת צְדָקָה וּמִשְׁפָּט 19c

לְמַעַן הָבִיא יְהוָה עַל־אַבְרָהָם אֵת אֲשֶׁר־דִּבֶּר עָלָיו: 19d

19a   Part-**V**
19b   Part-Rel-**V-O**-PP
19c   **V-O**-Compl
19d   Part-**V-S**-PP-Compl (Rel-**V**-PP)

וַיֹּאמֶר יְהוָה 20a

זַעֲקַת סְדֹם וַעֲמֹרָה כִּי־רָבָּה 20b

וְחַטָּאתָם כִּי כָבְדָה מְאֹד: 20c

20a   **V-S**
20b   S-Part-**Pred**
20c   S-Part-**Pred**

אֵרֲדָה־נָּא 21a

וְאֶרְאֶה 21b

הַכְּצַעֲקָתָהּ הַבָּאָה אֵלַי עָשׂוּ כָּלָה 21c

וְאִם־לֹא אֵדָעָה: 21d

21a   **V**
21b   **V**
21c   Q-Casus Pendus (S-Ptcpl-PP)-**V-O**
21d   Part-Neg-**V**

22a וַיִּפְנוּ מִשָּׁם הָאֲנָשִׁים

22b וַיֵּלְכוּ סְדֹמָה

22c וְאַבְרָהָם עוֹדֶנּוּ עֹמֵד לִפְנֵי יְהוָה:

22a	**V-PP-S**
22b	**V**-AA
22c	**S**-PP-**V**(Ptcpl)-PP

23a וַיִּגַּשׁ אַבְרָהָם

23b וַיֹּאמַר

23c הַאַף תִּסְפֶּה צַדִּיק עִם־רָשָׁע:

23a	**V-S**
23b	**V**
23c	Q-Part-**V-O**-PP

24a אוּלַי יֵשׁ חֲמִשִּׁים צַדִּיקִם בְּתוֹךְ הָעִיר

24b הַאַף תִּסְפֶּה

24c וְלֹא־תִשָּׂא לַמָּקוֹם לְמַעַן חֲמִשִּׁים הַצַּדִּיקִם

24d אֲשֶׁר בְּקִרְבָּהּ:

24a	Part-**Pred-S**-PP
24b	Q-Part-**V**
24c	**V-O**-PP
24d	Rel-**Pred**(PP)

25a חָלִלָה לְּךָ מֵעֲשֹׂת כַּדָּבָר הַזֶּה

25b לְהָמִית צַדִּיק עִם־רָשָׁע

| 25a | Part-PP-Comp(Inf-PP) |
| 25b | Comp (Inf-**O**-PP) |

25c וְהָיָה כַצַּדִּיק כָּרָשָׁע חָלִלָה לָּךְ

25d הֲשֹׁפֵט כָּל־הָאָרֶץ לֹא יַעֲשֶׂה מִשְׁפָּט:

| 25c | **V-S**-PP-Part-PP |
| 25d | <u>Q-**S-V-O**</u> |

Moshavi does not treat v. 25d except to indicate that the interrogative particle is attached to a fronted subject.[19] This fronting is best

---

[19] Moshavi, *Word Order*, 79.

understood as a case of descriptive focusing.[20] Abraham has been questioning YHWH in regards to His planned actions against Sodom and Gomorrah. In doing this, Abraham has eschewed neutrality. His questioning in v. 25a indicates that he considers such a course of action improper or "unjust." The proposition "YHWH will do justice" is implied in the vv. 23–25. This fronting is a case of elaborating on who YHWH is, identifying Him as "the judge of all the earth."

26a וַיֹּאמֶר יְהֹוָה

26b אִם־אֶמְצָא בִסְדֹם חֲמִשִּׁים צַדִּיקִם בְּתוֹךְ הָעִיר

26c וְנָשָׂאתִי לְכָל־הַמָּקוֹם בַּעֲבוּרָם:

26a	**V-S**
26b	Part-**V**-PP-**O**-PP
26c	**V-O**-Part

27a וַיַּעַן אַבְרָהָם וַיֹּאמַר

27b הִנֵּה־נָא הוֹאַלְתִּי לְדַבֵּר אֶל־אֲדֹנָי

27c וְאָנֹכִי עָפָר וָאֵפֶר:

27a	**V-S-V**
27b	Part-**V**-Comp (Inf-PP)
27c	**S-Pred**

28a אוּלַי יַחְסְרוּן חֲמִשִּׁים הַצַּדִּיקִם חֲמִשָּׁה

28b הֲתַשְׁחִית בַּחֲמִשָּׁה אֶת־כָּל־הָעִיר

28a	Part-**V-S-O**
28b	Q-**V**-PP-**O**

28c וַיֹּאמֶר

28d לֹא אַשְׁחִית

28e אִם־אֶמְצָא שָׁם אַרְבָּעִים וַחֲמִשָּׁה:

28c	**V**
28d	**V**
28e	Part-**V**-Adv-**O**

---

[20] Ibid., 130–31.

29a וַיֹּסֶף עוֹד לְדַבֵּר אֵלָיו֙

29b וַיֹּאמַר

29c אוּלַי יִמָּצְאוּן שָׁם אַרְבָּעִים

29a V-Adv-Comp (Inf-PP)
29b V
29c Part-**V**-Adv-**S**

29d וַיֹּאמֶר֙

29e לֹא אֶעֱשֶׂה בַּעֲבוּר הָאַרְבָּעִים׃

29d V
29e **V**-PP

30a וַיֹּאמֶר

30b אַל־נָא יִחַר לַאדֹנָי֙

30c וַאֲדַבֵּרָה

30d אוּלַי יִמָּצְאוּן שָׁם שְׁלֹשִׁים

30a V
30b **V**-PP
30c V
30d Part-**V**-Adv-**S**

30e וַיֹּאמֶר֙

30f לֹא אֶעֱשֶׂה

30g אִם־אֶמְצָא שָׁם שְׁלֹשִׁים׃

30e V
30f V
30g Part-**V**-Adv-**O**

31a וַיֹּאמֶר

31b הִנֵּה־נָא הוֹאַלְתִּי לְדַבֵּר אֶל־אֲדֹנָי

31c אוּלַי יִמָּצְאוּן שָׁם עֶשְׂרִים

31a V
31b Part-**V**-Comp (Inf-PP)
31c Part-**V**-Adv-**S**

וַיֹּאמֶר 31d
לֹא אַשְׁחִית בַּעֲבוּר הָעֶשְׂרִים׃ 31e

31d   V
31e   V-PP

וַיֹּאמֶר 32a
אַל-נָא יִחַר לַאדֹנָי 32b
וַאֲדַבְּרָה אַךְ-הַפַּעַם 32c
אוּלַי יִמָּצְאוּן שָׁם עֲשָׂרָה 32d

32a   V
32b   V-PP
32c   V-Adv
32d   Part-V-Adv-S

וַיֹּאמֶר 32e
לֹא אַשְׁחִית בַּעֲבוּר הָעֲשָׂרָה׃ 32f

32e   V
32f   V-PP

וַיֵּלֶךְ יְהוָה 33a
כַּאֲשֶׁר כִּלָּה לְדַבֵּר אֶל-אַבְרָהָם 33b
וְאַבְרָהָם שָׁב לִמְקֹמוֹ׃ 33c

33a   V-S
33b   TempP[Rel-V-Comp(Inf PP)]
33c   **S-V-PP**

Wenham considers v. 33c to be the use of a circumstantial
clause to signal the end of an episode.[21] Moshavi considers v. 33c to
have 'Abraham' fronted for topicalization. She points out that the relationship between 'Abraham' and 'YHWH' is contextually created (the
two have been conversation partners) and topicalization does not need
to be between natural pairs. Abraham's actions are being compared to
YHWH's. Moshavi argues that this is an example of topicalization indicating similarity of action. The point is not to contrast Abraham and
YHWH as entities or to contrast their two different destinations.

---

[21] Wenham, *Genesis 26–50*, 38, following Andersen, *Sentence*, 81.

Hornkohl also notes that many clauses that have been called contrastive are not about highlighting differences between entities. He calls this type of topicalization, parallelization.[22] The point is the similarity of Abraham and YHWH's actions.[23] A translation representing the topicalization relationship might be, "YHWH departed just as he finished speaking to Abraham, and *similarly* Abraham returned to his place."

19:1a וַיָּבֹאוּ שְׁנֵי הַמַּלְאָכִים סְדֹמָה בָּעֶרֶב

1b וְלוֹט יֹשֵׁב בְּשַׁעַר־סְדֹם

19:1a **V-S**-AA-PP

1b **S-V**(Ptcpl)-PP

1c וַיַּרְא־לוֹט

1d וַיָּקָם לִקְרָאתָם

1e וַיִּשְׁתַּחוּ אַפַּיִם אָרְצָה:

1c **V-S**

1d **V**-Comp(inf)

1e **V**-Adv

2a וַיֹּאמֶר

2b הִנֶּה נָּא־אֲדֹנַי סוּרוּ נָא אֶל־בֵּית עַבְדְּכֶם

2c וְלִינוּ

2d וְרַחֲצוּ רַגְלֵיכֶם

2e וְהִשְׁכַּמְתֶּם

2f וַהֲלַכְתֶּם לְדַרְכְּכֶם

2a **V**

2b Part-Voc-**V**-PP

2c **V**

2d **V-O**

2e **V**

2f **V**-PP

---

[22] Hornkohl, "Pragmatics of the X-Verb Structure," 45–46.

[23] Moshavi, *Word Order*, 161.

וַיֹּאמְרוּ 2g

לֹא 2h

כִּי בָרְחוֹב נָלִין: 2i

2g   **V**

2h   Neg

2i   <u>Part-PP-**V**</u>

Wenham uses the general "emphasis" for the fronting in v. 2i.[24] This fronting would be classified as substitutional focusing in Moshavi's system.[25] In vv. 2a-b, Lot requests that the visitors "... turn aside to the house of your servant and spend the night..." This activates the proposition "You will spend the night at my house." The visitors wish to replace one of the variables in this proposition with a different one. In this case "the street" is supplied for "the house." "In the street" is fronted in order to mark it as the substituted focus.[26]

וַיִּפְצַר־בָּם מְאֹד 3a

וַיָּסֻרוּ אֵלָיו 3b

וַיָּבֹאוּ אֶל־בֵּיתוֹ 3c

3a   **V-O**-Adv

3b   **V**-PP

3c   **V**-PP

וַיַּעַשׂ לָהֶם מִשְׁתֶּה 3d

וּמַצּוֹת אָפָה 3e

וַיֹּאכֵלוּ: 3f

3d   **V**-IO-**O**

3e   **O-V**

3f   **V**

---

[24] Wenham, *Genesis 26–50*, 38.

[25] Moshavi, *Word Order*, 131–33.

[26] The preposition, being attached, is fronted even though strictly speaking it is not the focused element. Constituents are generally fronted as a whole, even when only part of the constituent is the focus proper (Moshavi, *Word Order,* 122–23).

Verse 3e is an example of Moshavi's topicalization. In commenting on
the relationships that obtain between items linked by topicalization,
Moshavi notes that this verse is an example of a "part-whole" set for
the two relevant constituents.[27] "Unleavened bread" is part of "a
feast." Moshavi does not state a categorization for this verse, but given
the relationship between the linked items, it falls into the category of
topicalization for elaboration.[28] Lot "baking unleavened bread" is part
of what it means that "He prepared a feast for them."

Topicalization for elaboration is preferable to Hornkohl's classification of this clause as conveying simultaneity. Even he is hesitant
to give said label to v. 3e and notes the possibility that this clause is
explanatory of the previous clause.[29] The point of the elaboration is a
contrast between the meager offering of Lot (though it is called a
"feast") and the extravagant offering of Abraham earlier in chapter
18.[30]

4a טֶרֶם יִשְׁכָּבוּ

4b וְאַנְשֵׁי הָעִיר אַנְשֵׁי סְדֹם נָסַבּוּ עַל־הַבַּיִת מִנַּעַר וְעַד־זָקֵן כָּל־הָעָם מִקָּצֶה:

4a   Adv-V
4b   <u>S-V-PP-Right-Dislocation (PP-PP-S-PP)</u>

Moshavi does not discuss v. 4b, except to note the interesting
right dislocation.[31] The clause is either part of unexplained residue or
starting a new scene. Reasons to consider the clause unexplained include: the clause has a modifying temporal clause preceding it, and the
temporal clause is better understood as starting the new scene. The
temporal phrase in v. 4a connects what follows closely with what has
preceded. "Before they lay down," i.e., "While they were in the midst

---

[27] Moshavi, *Word Order*, 148.

[28] Ibid., 162–63.

[29] Hornkohl, "Pragmatics of the X-Verb Structure," 64.

[30] On the nature of Abraham's provisions see Nahum M. Sarna, *The JPS
Torah Commentary: Genesis* (Philadelphia: Jewish Publication Society of America,
1989), 129; and Wenham 26–50, *Genesis,* 11.

[31] Moshavi, *Word Order*, 68.

of settling in." Alternatively, this a scene transition. The pictured setting changes from what is happening in Lot's house to what is happening outside it. This understanding would coincide with Hornkohl's
concept of "intra-episode scene switching."[32]

5a וַיִּקְרְאוּ אֶל־לוֹט וַיֹּאמְרוּ לוֹ

5b אַיֵּה הָאֲנָשִׁים

5c אֲשֶׁר־בָּאוּ אֵלֶיךָ הַלָּיְלָה

5d הוֹצִיאֵם אֵלֵינוּ

5e וְנֵדְעָה אֹתָם:

5a	V-PP-V-PP
5b	Q-S
5c	Rel-V-PP-AA
5d	V-PP
5e	**V-O**

6a וַיֵּצֵא אֲלֵהֶם לוֹט הַפֶּתְחָה

6b וְהַדֶּלֶת סָגַר אַחֲרָיו:

| 6a | V-PP-S-AA |
| 6b | **O-V-PP** |

Moshavi lists v. 6b among the cases of topicalization where the
purpose is difficult to identify.[33] The most obvious candidates for the
linked items are the fronted "door" and the "entrance" of the previous
clause. Like v. 3e, Moshavi sees the logical relationship between the
two items as "part-whole" or "A has a B." Wenham sees this as a circumstantial clause closing the paragraph.[34] This identification is du-
bious by its lack of consistency in application. It is not apparent how
one would substantiate it. Stephen Levinsohn has suggested that
"door" is topicalized in order to highlight the importance of what follows. In this case the topicalization is in order to highlight Lot's response in v. 7.[35]

---

[32] Hornkohl, "Pragmatics of the X-Verb Structure," 70.

[33] Moshavi, *Word Order*, 155.

[34] Wenham, *Genesis 26–50*, 38.

[35] Stephen H. Levinsohn, "Unmarked and Marked Instances of Topicalization in Hebrew" in *Work Papers of the Summer Institute of Linguistics, University of*

7a וַיֹּאמֶר

7b אַל־נָא אַחַי תָּרֵעוּ׃

7a   **V**

7b   Neg-Voc-**V**

8a הִנֵּה־נָא לִי שְׁתֵּי בָנוֹת

8b   אֲשֶׁר לֹא־יָדְעוּ אִישׁ

8a   Part-**Pred** (PP)-S

8b   Rel-**V**-S

8c אוֹצִיאָה־נָּא אֶתְהֶן אֲלֵיכֶם

8d וַעֲשׂוּ לָהֶן כַּטּוֹב בְּעֵינֵיכֶם

8c   **V-O**-PP

8d   **V**-PP-PP

8e רַק לָאֲנָשִׁים הָאֵל אַל־תַּעֲשׂוּ דָבָר

8f   כִּי־עַל־כֵּן בָּאוּ בְּצֵל קֹרָתִי׃

8e   Part-PP-**V-O**

8f   Part-**V**-PP

9a וַיֹּאמְרוּ

9b גֶּשׁ־הָלְאָה

9a   **V**

9b   **V**-Adv

9c וַיֹּאמְרוּ

9d הָאֶחָד בָּא

9e   לָגוּר

9f וַיִּשְׁפֹּט שָׁפוֹט

9g עַתָּה נָרַע לְךָ מֵהֶם

9c   **V**

9d   <u>**S-V**</u>

9e   **V**(Inf)

9f   **V**

9g   Adv-**V**-PP-PP

North Dakota Sessions, eds., Robert A. Dooley and J. Albert Bickford (Dallas: SIL International, 1990), 29–30.

Moshavi does not discuss v. 9d. The clause is either residue or an example of topicalization for expressing similarity. "This one (Lot)" is being compared to the previously mentioned visitors. The visitors were the subject of the Sodomites' original request and remained active topics in Lot's reply. Furthermore, the visitors are mentioned abruptly at the end of the Sodomites' reply when they say, "Now we will do worse to you than to *them*." This can also be considered a case of forward topicalization.[36] The point is that Lot is also a sojourner, just like the two men. Lot is acting as buffer between the Sodomites and the two sojourners. Lot is fronted in the men's response to indicate that it is absurd for him to do so, as he too is a sojourner.

9h וַיִּפְצְרוּ בָאִישׁ בְּלוֹט מְאֹד

9i וַיִּגְּשׁוּ לִשְׁבֹּר הַדָּלֶת:

9h	**V-O**-App-Adv
9i	**V**-Compl (Inf-O)

10a וַיִּשְׁלְחוּ הָאֲנָשִׁים אֶת־יָדָם

10b וַיָּבִיאוּ אֶת־לוֹט אֲלֵיהֶם הַבָּיְתָה

10c וְאֶת־הַדֶּלֶת סָגָרוּ:

10a	**V-S-O**
10b	**V-O**-PP-AA
10c	<u>**O-V**</u>

Hornkohl highlights the similarity between the fronting here in v. 10c and in v. 6b earlier. He discusses the possibility that such frontings are used for dramatic pause, though he remains doubtful.[37]

Moshavi takes this as another example of a "part-whole" relationship between relevant constituents. She supposes that the purpose of such topicalization

> ... may be to ease the identification of "the door" which
> has a definite article, implying that it is identifiable,
> even though it is new to the discourse. Since a house

---

[36] Where the topicalized constituent is linked to a constituent in a following clause, rather than a preceding one. See Moshavi, *Word Order*, 151–52.

[37] Hornkohl, "Pragmatics of the X-Verb Structure," 71–73.

necessarily has a door, the reader can infer the existence of the door from the prior mention of the house. By linking "the door" to "the house," the topicalization cues the reader to make this inference.[38]

11a וְאֶת־הָאֲנָשִׁים אֲשֶׁר־פֶּתַח הַבַּיִת הִכּוּ בַּסַּנְוֵרִים מִקָּטֹן וְעַד־גָּדוֹל

11b וַיִּלְאוּ לִמְצֹא הַפָּתַח:

11a   **O** (O-Rel-AA) V-PP-PP-PP
11b   V-Compl (Inf-O)

Verse 11a involves a complex object constituent, consisting of the object itself and a relative clause modifying it. These have both been fronted before the verb. The two-part prepositional phrase at the end of the line, "from the smallest until the largest" modifies the object, but it has been moved to the end of the clause (right-dislocated). Moshavi does not comment on this verse except to note the use of both fronting and right-dislocation in the same clause.[39]

I propose understanding this as fronting for contrast. The contrast is between how the visitors acted upon Lot and how they acted on the Sodomites. The preceding verse narrates the actions of the angelic visitors in regards to Lot. They brought him into the house and shut the door. In contrast to how the visitors treat Lot (concern for his safety), they act as enemies of the Sodomites and protectors of Lot by striking them in such a way that they are unable to continue their pursuit of Lot. Victor Hamilton describes this as a juxtaposition of an act of salvation and an act of judgment.[40]

12a וַיֹּאמְרוּ הָאֲנָשִׁים אֶל־לוֹט

12b עֹד מִי־לְךָ פֹה

12c חָתָן וּבָנֶיךָ וּבְנֹתֶיךָ וְכֹל אֲשֶׁר־לְךָ בָּעִיר הוֹצֵא מִן־הַמָּקוֹם:

13a   כִּי־מַשְׁחִתִים אֲנַחְנוּ אֶת־הַמָּקוֹם הַזֶּה

13b   כִּי־גָדְלָה צַעֲקָתָם אֶת־פְּנֵי יְהוָה

13c   וַיְשַׁלְּחֵנוּ יְהוָה לְשַׁחֲתָהּ:

---

[38] Adina Moshavi, "Discourse Functions," 244.

[39] Moshavi, *Word Order*, 68.

[40] Hamilton, *Genesis*, 37.

12a   **V-S-PP**
12b   Adv-Q-PP-Adv
12c   **O-V-PP**
13a   Part-**V**(ptcpl)-**S-O**
13b   Part-**V-S**-PP
13c   **V**(**V-O**)-**S**-Comp [Inf (Inf-O)]

Verse 12c involves the fronting of an object. While Moshavi does not discuss this verse (except to point out that fronting can occur with imperatives)[41] this is best understood as a case of fronting for descriptive focusing.[42] In the previous line, the visitors ask Lot, "Who do you have left here?" This activates the proposition "You have X left here." The fronted constituent supplies further suggestive examples of the ones that might fill the X slot, "sons-in-law, daughters, sons, and anyone else . . ."

14a וַיֵּצֵ֣א ל֗וֹט
14b וַיְדַבֵּ֣ר ׀ אֶל־חֲתָנָ֣יו ׀
14c לֹקְחֵ֣י בְנֹתָ֗יו
14d וַיֹּ֙אמֶר֙

14a   **V-S**
14b   V-PP
14c   **V**(ptcpl)-**O**
14d   V

14e קֽוּמוּ צְּא֞וּ מִן־הַמָּק֤וֹם הַזֶּ֔ה
14f כִּֽי־מַשְׁחִ֥ית יְהוָ֖ה אֶת־הָעִ֑יר
14g וַיְהִ֥י כִמְצַחֵ֖ק בְּעֵינֵ֥י חֲתָנָֽיו׃

14e   **V-V**-PP
14f   Part-**V**(ptcpl)-**S-O**
14g   V-PP-PP

15a וּכְמוֹ֙ הַשַּׁ֣חַר עָלָ֔ה
15b וַיָּאִ֥יצוּ הַמַּלְאָכִ֖ים בְּל֣וֹט לֵאמֹ֑ר

15a   <u>Prep-S-V</u>
15b   **V-S-O**

---

[41] Moshavi, *Word Order*, 65.

[42] Ibid., 130–31.

   Verse 15a represents a clear case of subject fronting. It is a
temporal phrase, and we normally expect the author to have used an
infinitive with a prefixed כ. Instead the author places the subject between the verb and preposition, and uses the more rare independent
כְּמוֹ. The reason for such fronting is unclear. Presumably, the relationship between v. 15a and v. 15b is one of simultaneity or near-
simultaneity. However, this is just as easily achieved with the usual
infinitive + כ.

15c   קוּם קַח אֶת־אִשְׁתְּךָ וְאֶת־שְׁתֵּי בְנֹתֶיךָ

15d   הַנִּמְצָאֹת

15e   פֶּן־תִּסָּפֶה בַּעֲוֹן הָעִיר:

15c	**V-V-O**
15d	Ptcpl
15e	Part-**V**-PP

16a   וַיִּתְמַהְמָהּ׀

16b   וַיַּחֲזִקוּ הָאֲנָשִׁים בְּיָדוֹ וּבְיַד־אִשְׁתּוֹ וּבְיַד שְׁתֵּי בְנֹתָיו בְּחֶמְלַת יְהוָה עָלָיו

16c   וַיֹּצִאֻהוּ

16d   וַיַּנִּחֻהוּ מִחוּץ לָעִיר:

16a	**V**
16b	**V-S-O**-PP
16c	**V**(V-O)
16d	**V**(V-O)-PP

17a   וַיְהִי כְהוֹצִיאָם אֹתָם הַחוּצָה

17b   וַיֹּאמֶר

17a	TempP(**V**-PP-**O**-AA)
17b	**V**

17c   הִמָּלֵט עַל־נַפְשֶׁךָ

17d   אַל־תַּבִּיט אַחֲרֶיךָ

17e   וְאַל־תַּעֲמֹד בְּכָל־הַכִּכָּר הָהָרָה

17f   הִמָּלֵט

17g   פֶּן־תִּסָּפֶה:

17c	**V-PP**
17d	**V-PP**
17e	**V-PP-AA**
17f	**V**
17g	Part-**V**

18a וַיֹּאמֶר לוֹט אֲלֵהֶם
18b אַל־נָא אֲדֹנָי:

18a	**V-S-PP**
18b	Neg-Voc

19a הִנֵּה־נָא מָצָא עַבְדְּךָ חֵן בְּעֵינֶיךָ
19b וַתַּגְדֵּל חַסְדְּךָ
19c אֲשֶׁר עָשִׂיתָ עִמָּדִי
19d לְהַחֲיוֹת אֶת־נַפְשִׁי

19a	Part-**V-S-O**-PP
19b	**V-O**
19c	Rel-V-PP
19d	**V**(Inf)-**S**

19e וְאָנֹכִי לֹא אוּכַל לְהִמָּלֵט הָהָרָה
19f פֶּן־תִּדְבָּקַנִי הָרָעָה
19g וָמַתִּי:

19e	<u>**S-V**-Comp (Inf-AA)</u>
19f	Part-**V**(V-O)-**S**
19g	**V**

Moshavi and Hornkohl do not comment on the fronting in this verse. There are two options here. Verse 19e could be a case of focusing for identification. If the messengers' command to escape included the idea of escaping to the mountains (which would be part of their shared world knowledge of the area) then "You will go to the mountain" as well as the negative "X cannot go to the mountain" are considered active. Lot emphasizes his inability to do so with the presence of the pronoun.

Alternatively, the fronting can be understood as a forward-linking topicalization of opposition. The linked items are Lot and the impending disaster (רָעָה). The pair are linked contextually and the comparison is the movement of both. Lot compares his inability to escape to the mountains with the disaster's ability to overtake him. The result would be a pleasing play on concepts. "I cannot reach the mountains, but the disaster can reach me."

20a הִנֵּה־נָא הָעִיר הַזֹּאת קְרֹבָה לָנוּס שָׁמָּה
20b וְהִיא מִצְעָר

20a   Part-**S-Pred**(Adj-Inf-Adv)
20b   **S-Pred**

20c אִמָּלְטָה נָּא שָׁמָּה
20d הֲלֹא מִצְעָר הִוא
20e וּתְחִי נַפְשִׁי׃

20c   V-Adv
20d   Q-**Pred-S**
20e   V-S

21a וַיֹּאמֶר אֵלָיו
21b הִנֵּה נָשָׂאתִי פָנֶיךָ
21c גַּם לַדָּבָר הַזֶּה
21d לְבִלְתִּי הָפְכִּי אֶת־הָעִיר
21e אֲשֶׁר דִּבַּרְתָּ׃

21a   **V**-PP
21b   Part-**V-O**
21c   Part-PP
21d   InfP(Neg-Inf-Subj)-**O**
21e   Rel-**V**

22a מַהֵר הִמָּלֵט שָׁמָּה
22b כִּי לֹא אוּכַל לַעֲשׂוֹת דָּבָר עַד־בֹּאֲךָ שָׁמָּה
22c עַל־כֵּן קָרָא שֵׁם־הָעִיר צוֹעַר׃

22a   **V-V**-Adv
22b   Part-**V**-Comp(Inf-O)-PP
22c   Part-**V-O-O**

23a הַשֶּׁמֶשׁ יָצָא עַל־הָאָרֶץ

23b וְלוֹט בָּא צֹעֲרָה:

24 וַיהוָה הִמְטִיר עַל־סְדֹם וְעַל־עֲמֹרָה גָּפְרִית וָאֵשׁ מֵאֵת יְהוָה מִן־הַשָּׁמָיִם:

23a	**S-V-PP**
23b	**S-V-AA**
24	**S-V-PP-O-PP-PP**

Verses 23–24 are interesting complex of three fronted clauses. Moshavi considers all three to be part of the residue (not topicalizing or focusing the fronted constituent). She takes these to be clauses marked by fronting and conveying simultaneity.[43] The point of this construction is that Lot arrived at Zoar as YHWH was raining fire down on Sodom and Gomorrah, and that both of these happened at sunrise.

25 וַיַּהֲפֹךְ אֶת־הֶעָרִים הָאֵל וְאֵת כָּל־הַכִּכָּר וְאֵת כָּל־יֹשְׁבֵי הֶעָרִים וְצֶמַח הָאֲדָמָה:

25	**V-O**

26a וַתַּבֵּט אִשְׁתּוֹ מֵאַחֲרָיו

26b וַתְּהִי נְצִיב מֶלַח:

26a	**V-S-PP**
26b	**V-Pred**

27a וַיַּשְׁכֵּם אַבְרָהָם בַּבֹּקֶר אֶל־הַמָּקוֹם

27b אֲשֶׁר־עָמַד שָׁם אֶת־פְּנֵי יְהוָה:

27a	**V-S-PP-PP**
27b	Rel-**V**-Adv-PP

28a וַיַּשְׁקֵף עַל־פְּנֵי סְדֹם וַעֲמֹרָה וְעַל־כָּל־פְּנֵי אֶרֶץ הַכִּכָּר

28b וַיַּרְא

28c וְהִנֵּה עָלָה קִיטֹר הָאָרֶץ כְּקִיטֹר הַכִּבְשָׁן:

28a	**V-PP**
28b	**V**
28c	Part-**V-S-PP-PP**

---

[43] Moshavi, *Word Order*, 113–14.

29a וַיְהִ֗י בְּשַׁחֵ֤ת אֱלֹהִים֙ אֶת־עָרֵ֣י הַכִּכָּ֔ר

29b וַיִּזְכֹּ֥ר אֱלֹהִ֖ים אֶת־אַבְרָהָ֑ם

29a TempP[V-PP(Prep-Inf-**S-O**)]

29b **V-S-O**

29c וַיְשַׁלַּ֤ח אֶת־לוֹט֙ מִתּ֣וֹךְ הַהֲפֵכָ֔ה

29d בַּהֲפֹךְ֙ אֶת־הֶ֣עָרִ֔ים

29e אֲשֶׁר־יָשַׁ֥ב בָּהֵ֖ן לֽוֹט׃

29c **V-O**-PP

29d TempP (Prep-Inf-**O**)

29e Rel-**V**-PP-**S**

30a וַיַּ֩עַל֩ ל֨וֹט מִצּ֜וֹעַר

30a **V-S-PP**

30b וַיֵּ֣שֶׁב בָּהָ֔ר

30c וּשְׁתֵּ֤י בְנֹתָיו֙ עִמּ֔וֹ

30d כִּ֥י יָרֵ֖א לָשֶׁ֣בֶת בְּצ֑וֹעַר

30b **V**-PP

30c **S-Pred**(PP)

30d Part-**V**-Comp(Inf-PP)

30e וַיֵּ֙שֶׁב֙ בַּמְּעָרָ֔ה ה֖וּא וּשְׁתֵּ֥י בְנֹתָֽיו׃

30e **V**-PP-Right Dislocation

31a וַתֹּ֧אמֶר הַבְּכִירָ֛ה אֶל־הַצְּעִירָ֖ה

31a **V-S-PP**

31b אָבִ֣ינוּ זָקֵ֑ן

31c וְאִ֨ישׁ אֵ֤ין בָּאָ֙רֶץ֙ לָב֣וֹא עָלֵ֔ינוּ כְּדֶ֖רֶךְ כָּל־הָאָֽרֶץ׃

31b **S-Pred**

31c **S-Pred** (Part-PP)-Comp (Inf-PP-PP)

If זָקֵן is taken as an adjective then the word order of v. 31b is standard. However, if it is taken as a verb, the subject would be fronted. There is no apparent reason for the fronting in this address, so rather than include this clause in Moshavi's unexplained residue it is simpler to take זָקֵן as an adjective.

לְכָה נַשְׁקֶה אֶת־אָבִינוּ יַיִן 32a
וְנִשְׁכְּבָה עִמּוֹ 32b
וּנְחַיֶּה מֵאָבִינוּ זָרַע׃ 32c

32a   **V-V-O-O**
32b   **V-PP**
32c   **V-PP-O**

וַתַּשְׁקֶיןָ אֶת־אֲבִיהֶן יַיִן בַּלַּיְלָה הֽוּא 33a
וַתָּבֹא הַבְּכִירָה 33b
וַתִּשְׁכַּב אֶת־אָבִיהָ 33c
וְלֹא־יָדַע בְּשִׁכְבָהּ וּבְקוּמָהּ׃ 33d

33a   **V-O-O**-PP
33b   **V-S**
33c   **V-PP**
33d   **V**-Compl (PP-PP)

וַיְהִי מִֽמָּחֳרָת 34a
וַתֹּאמֶר הַבְּכִירָה אֶל־הַצְּעִירָה 34b

34a   TempP(**V-PP**)
34b   **V-S**-PP

הֵן־שָׁכַבְתִּי אֶמֶשׁ אֶת־אָבִי 34c
נַשְׁקֶנּוּ יַיִן גַּם־הַלַּיְלָה 34d

34c   Part-**V**-Adv-PP
34d   **V-O**-Adv

וּבֹאִי שִׁכְבִי עִמּוֹ 34e
וּנְחַיֶּה מֵאָבִינוּ זָרַע׃ 34f

34e   **V-V**-PP
34f   **V-PP-O**

וַתַּשְׁקֶיןָ גַּם בַּלַּיְלָה הַהוּא אֶת־אֲבִיהֶן יָיִן 35a
וַתָּקָם הַצְּעִירָה 35b
וַתִּשְׁכַּב עִמּוֹ 35c
וְלֹא־יָדַע בְּשִׁכְבָהּ וּבְקֻמָהּ׃ 35d

35a   **V**-Adv-**O-O**
35b   **V-S**
35c   **V-PP**
35d   **V**-Comp (PP-PP)

36a וַתַּהֲרֶיןָ שְׁתֵּי בְנוֹת־לוֹט מֵאֲבִיהֶן׃

36a   **V-S**-PP

37a וַתֵּלֶד הַבְּכִירָה בֵּן
37b וַתִּקְרָא שְׁמוֹ מוֹאָב

37a   **V-S-O**
37b   **V-O-O**

37c הוּא אֲבִי־מוֹאָב עַד־הַיּוֹם׃

37c   **S-Pred**-PP

38a וְהַצְּעִירָה גַם־הִוא יָלְדָה בֵּן
38b וַתִּקְרָא שְׁמוֹ בֶּן־עַמִּי
38c הוּא אֲבִי בְנֵי־עַמּוֹן עַד־הַיּוֹם׃ ס

38a   <u>S</u>-Adv-**V-O**
38b   **V-O-O**
38c   **S-Pred**-PP

The fronting in v. 38a is a clear case of additive focusing, given the presence of גַם־הִוא.. If the particle and 3FS pronoun were omitted, one would understand this as a case of topicalization expressing similarity. There is little difference between the two in this case.

5.4. Summary

In the Sodom episode we observe twenty-four examples of fronting. Fourteen have the subject fronted. Five have the object fronted. Four have a prepositional phrase fronted. In only one case is a participle fronted. Every case where a prepositional phrase is fronted represents a clear example of focusing in Moshavi's information structure. With arguably four out of five cases, object focusing seems to be more commonly used for topicalization. Subject fronting serves the most varied purposes, and only subject fronting seems to indicate a particular discourse role for the clause as a whole. Subject fronting for reasons other than topicalization or focusing represents the majority of cases (eight out of fourteen).

Chapter 6
GENESIS 18–19: A SVO COMMENTARY

This chapter will present a graphically laid out syntactic outline of Gen 18–19 with word order relevant labels and commentary. The commentary will assume an SVO view and apply Robert Holmstedt's information structure.

6.1. Word Order Labels
The labeling is essentially the same as in the previous chapter. Clauses that are considered to have a pragmatically marked constituent or that are experiencing semantically triggered inversion are under-lined.[1]

6.2. Sodom Commentary: SVO

18:1a וַיֵּרָא אֵלָיו יְהוָה בְּאֵלֹנֵי מַמְרֵא
1b וְהוּא יֹשֵׁב פֶּתַח־הָאֹהֶל כְּחֹם הַיּוֹם:

18:1a   **V-IO-S-PP**
1b   **S-V(Ptcpl)-AA-PP**

2a וַיִּשָּׂא עֵינָיו
2b וַיַּרְא
2c וְהִנֵּה שְׁלֹשָׁה אֲנָשִׁים נִצָּבִים עָלָיו

2a   **V-O**
2b   **V**
2c   Part-**S**-V(Ptcpl)-PP

2d וַיַּרְא וַיָּרָץ לִקְרָאתָם מִפֶּתַח הָאֹהֶל
2e וַיִּשְׁתַּחוּ אָרְצָה:

2d   **V-V-Comp-PP**
2e   **V-AA**

---

[1] That is, marked by fronting a constituent to the beginning of a clause. Post-verbal fronting, left-dislocation, and right-dislocation, as well as other forms of marking are outside the scope of this work.

3a וַיֹּאמַ֑ר

3b אֲדֹנָ֗י אִם־נָ֨א מָצָ֤אתִי חֵן֙ בְּעֵינֶ֔יךָ

3c אַל־נָ֥א תַעֲבֹ֖ר מֵעַ֥ל עַבְדֶּֽךָ׃

3a   V
3b   Voc-**V-O**-PP
3c   **V**-PP

4a יֻקַּֽח־נָ֣א מְעַט־מַ֔יִם

4b וְרַחֲצ֖וּ רַגְלֵיכֶ֑ם

4c וְהִֽשָּׁעֲנ֖וּ תַּ֥חַת הָעֵֽץ׃

4a   <u>**V-S**</u>
4b   **V-O**
4c   **V**-PP

The irrealis sense of the verb causes the clause to exhibit VS order. יֻקַּח can be recognized as a jussive by the inclusion of the נָא particle. The position of the verb is expected given its semantic value. This means יֻקַּח would still be recognized as an irrealis verb apart from the inclusion of the נָא particle.

5a וְאֶקְחָ֨ה פַת־לֶ֜חֶם

5b וְסַעֲד֤וּ לִבְּכֶם֙

5c אַחַ֣ר תַּעֲבֹ֔רוּ

5d כִּֽי־עַל־כֵּ֥ן עֲבַרְתֶּ֖ם עַֽל־עַבְדְּכֶ֑ם

5a   **V-O**
5b   **V-S**
5c   PP-**V**
5d   Part(Part-PP)-**V-O**

5e וַיֹּ֣אמְר֔וּ

5f כֵּ֥ן תַּעֲשֶׂ֖ה

5g כַּאֲשֶׁ֥ר דִּבַּֽרְתָּ׃

5e   V
5f   Part-**V**
5g   Rel-**V**

6a וַיְמַהֵר אַבְרָהָם הָאֹהֱלָה אֶל־שָׂרָה

6b וַיֹּאמֶר

6a   **V-S-AA-PP**

6b   **V**

6c מַהֲרִי שְׁלֹשׁ סְאִים קֶמַח סֹלֶת

6d לוּשִׁי וַעֲשִׂי עֻגוֹת:

6c   **V-O**

6d   **V-V-O**

7a וְאֶל־הַבָּקָר רָץ אַבְרָהָם

7b וַיִּקַּח בֶּן־בָּקָר רַךְ וָטוֹב

7c וַיִּתֵּן אֶל־הַנַּעַר

7d וַיְמַהֵר לַעֲשׂוֹת אֹתוֹ:

7a   <u>**PP-V-S**</u>

7b   **V-O**

7c   **V-PP**

7d   **V-Comp**

Verse 7a has a fronted PP. The following VS order is not the result of fronting but of triggered inversion following the fronted PP. The PP can be considered a topic. However, "the cattle" are not a thematic element as they have not even been hinted at previously in the discourse. The only topic function could be setting the scene, but the place of the cattle does not seem to be the purpose of their being mentioned.[2] It is best to understand the fronted PP as marking focus. "To the cattle" is being contrasted with the presumed itinerary of Sarah. Abraham had given her instructions to make cakes in vv. 6c-d. Her destination in is implicitly active in the mind of the readers (i.e., Sarah went off to the cupboard/kitchen/storeroom). "To the cattle" is fronted to contrast Abraham's destination with Sarah's.

---

[2] For the two basic functions of topic, Robert Holmstedt, "Word Order and Information Structure," 128.

8a וַיִּקַּח חֶמְאָה וְחָלָב וּבֶן־הַבָּקָר֙

8b   אֲשֶׁר עָשָׂה

8c וַיִּתֵּן לִפְנֵיהֶם

8a **V-O**

8b   Rel-**V**

8c **V**-PP

8d וְהוּא־עֹמֵד עֲלֵיהֶם תַּחַת הָעֵץ

8e וַיֹּאכֵלוּ׃

8d **S-V**(Ptcpl)-PP-PP

8e **V**

9a וַיֹּאמְרוּ אֵלָיו

9b אַיֵּה שָׂרָה אִשְׁתֶּךָ

9a **V**-PP

9b Q-**S**-(S-App)

9c וַיֹּאמֶר

9d הִנֵּה בָאֹהֶל׃

9c **V**

9d Part-PP

10a וַיֹּאמֶר

10b שׁוֹב אָשׁוּב אֵלֶיךָ֙ כָּעֵת חַיָּה

10c וְהִנֵּה־בֵן לְשָׂרָה אִשְׁתֶּךָ

10a **V**

10b **V**-PP-PP

10c Part-**S-Pred** (PP-App)

10d וְשָׂרָה שֹׁמַעַת פֶּתַח הָאֹהֶל

10e וְהוּא אַחֲרָיו׃

10d **S-V**(ptcpl)-AA

10e **S-Pred**(PP)

11a וְאַבְרָהָם וְשָׂרָה זְקֵנִים
11b בָּאִים בַּיָּמִים
11c חָדַל לִהְיוֹת לְשָׂרָה אֹרַח כַּנָּשִׁים:

11a	**S-Pred**
11b	**V(Ptcpl)-PP**
11c	<u>**V-PP-S**</u>

Verse 11c has no syntactic operators that would result in VS order. In context the verb does not make sense as an irreal perfect. "It ceased" has been fronted as either a topic or focus. It clearly does not give a setting, nor is "it ceased" thematic. The verb cannot be a topic and must be focus fronted.

There are two possibilities for what "it ceased" might be contrasted with. English versions, such as the ESV usually render the second line something like, "advanced in age." However, it is literally a participial phrase, "going (on) in the days." The verb בוא can be understood as opposed to חָדַל. If this is in fact the intended contrast, it is a play on movement imagery by the author. "Abraham and Sarah were advancing in age, <u>but</u> the way of women had stopped in Sarah."

Alternatively, חָדַל may be contrasted with it's logical opposite "continuing." "The way of the women had stopped for Sarah." A marked interpretation of חָדַל is attractive in context. Sarah's inability to have children is a central feature of this and following narratives.

12a וַתִּצְחַק שָׂרָה בְּקִרְבָּהּ לֵאמֹר
12b אַחֲרֵי בְלֹתִי הָיְתָה־לִּי עֶדְנָה
12c וַאדֹנִי זָקֵן:

12a	V-S-PP
12b	TempP[Prep-V(Inf)]-V-PP-S
12c	**S-V**

Verse 12c is best understood as a basic SV clause in direct discourse. "My Lord" is not being contrasted with another younger person and though it might be considered thematic, there are no other available themes to be the subject of זָקֵן. Topic marking does not "function redundantly" to mark a theme when there are no options of multiple themes.[3]

13a וַיֹּאמֶר יְהוָה אֶל־אַבְרָהָם

13b לָמָּה זֶּה צָחֲקָה שָׂרָה לֵאמֹר

13c הַאַף אָמְנָם אֵלֵד

13d וַאֲנִי זָקַנְתִּי

13a   **V-S-IO**
13b   **Q-V-S**
13c   **Q-Part-V**
13d   **<u>S-V</u>**

Verse 13d includes an explicit subject in the form of a personal pronoun. In contrast to the previous verse, this is best understood as a case of the subject being marked as a topic. The surface order is what one would expect, but the inclusion of the 1st person personal pronoun merits explanation. Holmstedt notes that personal pronouns are usually included as a topic marker and not a focus marker.[4] If the pronoun were a focus here, one would expect the context to have an entity which was young, to be contrasted with Sarah. Though there are no other possible themes that would agree with the verb in person and number, the previous words by Sarah in v. 12b and v. 12c spoke of Abraham's age. In YHWH's speech, the 1CS pronoun (representing Sarah, as YHWH is speaking from her point of view) is fronted to select Sarah and not Abraham as the topic of of the "age complaint," highlighting the fact that in her mind, her age was also a factor in her incredulity.

An attractive alternative is that the inclusion of the pronoun can be for the purpose of preserving SV order and thus an indicative understanding of the clause. Without the pronoun a *weqatal* form would be produced.[5]

---

[3] Holmstedt, "Word Order and Information Structure," 130.

[4] Ibid., 131.

[5] I am indebted to my thesis supervisor, Eric J. Tully, for this suggestion.

הֲיִפָּלֵא מֵיהוָה דָּבָר 14a
לַמּוֹעֵד אָשׁוּב אֵלֶיךָ כָּעֵת חַיָּה 14b
וּלְשָׂרָה בֵן׃ 14c

14a Q-V-PP-**S**
14b <u>PP-V-PP-PP</u>
14c **Pred(PP)-S**

   Verses 14b and 14c both contain a fronted PP. The first fronted PP is an example of the topic function of setting the scene. The second fronted PP is an example of fronting for focus. "To Sarah" is being contrasted with the remaining members of the logical set {all women}. Sarah, as opposed the myriads of women in existence, would be visited by YHWH and she would receive a son.

וַתְּכַחֵשׁ שָׂרָה׀ לֵאמֹר 15a
לֹא צָחַקְתִּי 15b
כִּי׀ יָרֵאָה 15c

15a **V-S**
15b **V**
15c   Part-**V**

וַיֹּאמֶר׀ 15d
לֹא כִּי צָחָקְתְּ׃ 15e

15d **V**
15e Neg-Part-**V**

וַיָּקֻמוּ מִשָּׁם הָאֲנָשִׁים 16a
וַיַּשְׁקִפוּ עַל־פְּנֵי סְדֹם 16b
וְאַבְרָהָם הֹלֵךְ עִמָּם 16c
לְשַׁלְּחָם׃ 16d

16a **V**-PP-**S**
16b **V**-PP
16c S-**V**(Ptcpl)-PP
16d   **V**

17a וַיהֹוָה אָמָר

17b הַמְכַסֶּה אֲנִי מֵאַבְרָהָם

17c אֲשֶׁר אֲנִי עֹשֶׂה׃

17a   **S-V**

17b   Q-V(Ptcpl)-**S**-PP

17c   Rel-**S**-**V**(Ptcpl)

The SV order of v. 17a is expected. However, the position of the subject also represents a pragmatic marking. YHWH is marked as the topic by fronting. YHWH is being selected from Abraham, the men, and YHWH as the carrying forward the next section.

Participles do not undergo triggered inversion and thus the participle in v. 17b has been fronted.[6] The fronting focuses on the participle, contrasting it with its logical opposite, "to reveal." This contrast explicitly makes this a rhetorical question. The sense is, "Shall I hide and not reveal what I am about to do from Abraham?"

18a וְאַבְרָהָם הָיוֹ יִהְיֶה לְגוֹי גָּדוֹל וְעָצוּם

18b וְנִבְרְכוּ בוֹ כֹּל גּוֹיֵי הָאָרֶץ׃

18a   **S-V**-Compl

18b   **V**-PP-**S**

The SV order is expected. However, the position of the subject also represents a pragmatic marking. Abraham and YHWH are both active themes in the YHWH's speech. The fronted subject is topic marking. The VS order in v. 18b signals that the verb is to be understood as irreal.

19a כִּי יְדַעְתִּיו

19b לְמַעַן אֲשֶׁר יְצַוֶּה אֶת־בָּנָיו וְאֶת־בֵּיתוֹ אַחֲרָיו

19c וְשָׁמְרוּ דֶּרֶךְ יְהֹוָה לַעֲשׂוֹת צְדָקָה וּמִשְׁפָּט

19d לְמַעַן הָבִיא יְהֹוָה עַל־אַבְרָהָם אֵת אֲשֶׁר־דִּבֶּר עָלָיו׃

19a   Part-**V**

19b   Part-Rel-**V**-**O**-PP

19c   **V**-**O**-Compl

19d   Part-**V**-**S**-PP-Compl (Rel-**V**-PP)

---

[6] Holmstedt, "Relative Clause," 157.

The verb is fronted over a null subject to indicate an irreal value. This means that the clause is understood as a representative of a VS clause. The subject is dropped, but the position of the verb is not considered the result of the lack of a subject.

20a וַיֹּאמֶר יְהוָה
20b זַעֲקַת סְדֹם וַעֲמֹרָה כִּי־רָבָּה
20c וְחַטָּאתָם כִּי כָבְדָה מְאֹד׃

20a	**V-S**
20b	S-Part-**Pred**
20c	S-Part-**Pred**

21a אֵרֲדָה־נָּא
21b וְאֶרְאֶה
21c הַכְּצַעֲקָתָהּ הַבָּאָה אֵלַי עָשׂוּ כָּלָה
21d וְאִם־לֹא אֵדָעָה׃

21a	**V**
21b	**V**
21c	Q-Casus Pendus (S-Ptcpl-PP)-**V-O**
21d	Part-Neg-**V**

22a וַיִּפְנוּ מִשָּׁם הָאֲנָשִׁים
22b וַיֵּלְכוּ סְדֹמָה
22c וְאַבְרָהָם עוֹדֶנּוּ עֹמֵד לִפְנֵי יְהוָה׃

22a	**V-PP-S**
22b	**V-AA**
22c	<u>S-PP-**V**(ptcpl)-PP</u>

The subject-participle order is expected in v. 22c. In this case, it represents a topic marking. Abraham, YHWH, and the men are all active discourse themes. The subject fronting serves to select and specify Abraham.

23a וַיִּגַּשׁ אַבְרָהָם
23b וַיֹּאמַר
23c הַאַף תִּסְפֶּה צַדִּיק עִם־רָשָׁע׃

23a	**V-S**
23b	**V**
23c	Q-Part-**V-O**-PP

אוּלַי יֵשׁ חֲמִשִּׁים צַדִּיקִם בְּתוֹךְ הָעִיר 24a

הַאַף תִּסְפֶּה 24b

וְלֹא־תִשָּׂא לַמָּקוֹם לְמַעַן חֲמִשִּׁים הַצַּדִּיקִם 24c

אֲשֶׁר בְּקִרְבָּהּ 24d

24a   Part-**Pred**-S-PP
24b   Q-Part-**V**
24c   **V-O**-PP
24d   Rel-**Pred**(PP)

חָלִלָה לְּךָ מֵעֲשֹׂת כַּדָּבָר הַזֶּה 25a

לְהָמִית צַדִּיק עִם־רָשָׁע 25b

25a   Part-PP-Comp(Inf-PP)
25b   Comp (Inf-**O**-PP)

וְהָיָה כַצַּדִּיק כָּרָשָׁע חָלִלָה לָּךְ 25c

הֲשֹׁפֵט כָּל־הָאָרֶץ לֹא יַעֲשֶׂה מִשְׁפָּט׃ 25d

25c   **V-S**-PP-Part-PP
25d   <u>Q-**S-V-O**</u>

The interrogative ה acts as a syntactic trigger and one would expect VSO order in v. 25d. However, here the subject has been fronted. "The judge of all the earth" is not thematic and cannot serve as a topic. The subject has been fronted as a focus. In this case "the judge of all the earth" is probably being contrasted with the remaining members of the logical set {all judges}. Therefore, the sense is, "If any judge were to do right in this situation, would it not be the judge of all the earth?"

וַיֹּאמֶר יְהֹוָה 26a

אִם־אֶמְצָא בִסְדֹם חֲמִשִּׁים צַדִּיקִם בְּתוֹךְ הָעִיר 26b

וְנָשָׂאתִי לְכָל־הַמָּקוֹם בַּעֲבוּרָם׃ 26c

26a   **V-S**
26b   Part-**V**-PP-**O**-PP
26c   <u>**V-O**-Part</u>

The verb in v. 26c is irreal. The subject has been dropped. The verb first order in the clause is a result of the irreal force and not the dropped subject. The assumed order of the clause if the subject were not dropped would be V-S-O-Part.

27a וַיַּעַן אַבְרָהָם וַיֹּאמַר
27b הִנֵּה־נָא הוֹאַלְתִּי לְדַבֵּר אֶל־אֲדֹנָי
27c וְאָנֹכִי עָפָר וָאֵפֶר:

27a	**V-S-V**
27b	Part-**V**-Comp (Inf-PP)
27c	**S-Pred**

28a אוּלַי יַחְסְרוּן חֲמִשִּׁים הַצַּדִּיקִם חֲמִשָּׁה
28b הֲתַשְׁחִית בַּחֲמִשָּׁה אֶת־כָּל־הָעִיר

28a	Part-**V-S-O**
28b	Q-**V**-PP-**O**

28c וַיֹּאמֶר
28d לֹא אַשְׁחִית
28e אִם־אֶמְצָא שָׁם אַרְבָּעִים וַחֲמִשָּׁה:

28c	**V**
28d	**V**
28e	Part-**V**-Adv-**O**

29a וַיֹּסֶף עוֹד לְדַבֵּר אֵלָיו
29b וַיֹּאמַר
29c אוּלַי יִמָּצְאוּן שָׁם אַרְבָּעִים

29a	**V**-Adv-Comp (Inf-PP)
29b	**V**
29c	Part-**V**-Adv-**S**

29d וַיֹּאמֶר
29e לֹא אֶעֱשֶׂה בַּעֲבוּר הָאַרְבָּעִים:

29d	**V**
29e	**V**-PP

30a וַיֹּאמֶר
30b אַל־נָא יִחַר לַאדֹנָי
30c וַאֲדַבֵּרָה
30d אוּלַי יִמָּצְאוּן שָׁם שְׁלֹשִׁים

30a   **V**
30b   **V**-PP
30c   **V**
30d   Part-**V**-Adv-**S**

30e וַיֹּאמֶר
30f לֹא אֶעֱשֶׂה
30g   אִם־אֶמְצָא שָׁם שְׁלֹשִׁים׃

30e   **V**
30f   **V**
30g   Part-**V**-Adv-**O**

31a וַיֹּאמֶר
31b הִנֵּה־נָא הוֹאַלְתִּי לְדַבֵּר אֶל־אֲדֹנָי
31c אוּלַי יִמָּצְאוּן שָׁם עֶשְׂרִים

31a   **V**
31b   Part-**V**-Comp (Inf-PP)
31c   Part-**V**-Adv-**S**

31d וַיֹּאמֶר
31e לֹא אַשְׁחִית בַּעֲבוּר הָעֶשְׂרִים׃

31d   **V**
31e   **V**-PP

32a וַיֹּאמֶר
32b אַל־נָא יִחַר לַאדֹנָי
32c וַאֲדַבְּרָה אַךְ־הַפַּעַם
32d אוּלַי יִמָּצְאוּן שָׁם עֲשָׂרָה

32a   **V**
32b   **V**-PP
32c   **V**-Adv
32d   Part-**V**-Adv-**S**

32e וַיֹּאמֶר
32f לֹא אַשְׁחִית בַּעֲבוּר הָעֲשָׂרָה׃

32e   **V**
32f   **V**-PP

33a וַיֵּלֶךְ יְהוָ֔ה

33b כַּאֲשֶׁ֣ר כִּלָּ֔ה לְדַבֵּ֖ר אֶל־אַבְרָהָ֑ם

33c וְאַבְרָהָ֖ם שָׁ֥ב לִמְקֹמֽוֹ׃

33a   **V-S**
33b   TempP[Rel-**V**-Comp(Inf PP)]
33c   <u>**S-V**-PP</u>

The SV word order of v. 33c is expected. However, the position of the subject should also be understood as fronted to mark it as a
topic. YHWH and Abraham have just been mentioned in the previous
half of the verse and are active themes. Abraham is selected as topic.

19:1a וַיָּבֹ֜אוּ שְׁנֵ֤י הַמַּלְאָכִים֙ סְדֹ֔מָה בָּעֶ֔רֶב

1b וְל֖וֹט יֹשֵׁ֣ב בְּשַֽׁעַר־סְדֹ֑ם

19:1a   **V-S**-AA-PP
1b   **S-V**(Ptcpl)-PP

1c וַיַּרְא־ל֗וֹט

1d וַיָּ֨קָם֙ לִקְרָאתָ֔ם

1e וַיִּשְׁתַּ֥חוּ אַפַּ֖יִם אָֽרְצָה׃

1c   **V-S**
1d   **V**-Comp(inf)
1e   **V**-Adv

2a וַיֹּ֕אמֶר

2b הִנֶּ֣ה נָּֽא־אֲדֹנַ֗י ס֣וּרוּ נָ֠א אֶל־בֵּ֨ית עַבְדְּכֶ֤ם

2c וְל֣ינוּ

2d וְרַחֲצ֣וּ רַגְלֵיכֶ֔ם

2e וְהִשְׁכַּמְתֶּ֖ם

2f וַהֲלַכְתֶּ֥ם לְדַרְכְּכֶ֑ם

2a   **V**
2b   Part-Voc-**V**-PP
2c   **V**
2d   **V-O**
2e   <u>**V**</u>
2f   <u>**V-PP**</u>[7]

---

[7] The verbs are understood as fronted over null subjects.

2g וַיֹּאמְר֖וּ
2h לֹ֔א
2i כִּ֥י בָרְח֖וֹב נָלִֽין׃

2g   **V**
2h   Neg
2i   Part-PP-**V**

The PP in v. 2i has been fronted over the verb as a focus. "In the street" is contrasting the previous suggestion. Lot had offered for the men to stay "in the house of your servant." The men's reply contrasts with Lot's as they offer an alternative lodging idea.

3a וַיִּפְצַר־בָּ֣ם מְאֹ֔ד
3b וַיָּסֻ֣רוּ אֵלָ֔יו
3c וַיָּבֹ֖אוּ אֶל־בֵּית֑וֹ

3a   **V-O**-Adv
3b   **V**-PP
3c   **V**-PP

3d וַיַּ֨עַשׂ לָהֶ֤ם מִשְׁתֶּה֙
3e וּמַצּ֣וֹת אָפָ֔ה
3f וַיֹּאכֵֽלוּ׃

3d   **V**-IO-**O**
3e   **O-V**
3f   **V**

The object in v. 3e has been fronted for focus. The "unleavened loaves" are selected from the logical set {things Lot could make for a feast} or in contrast to Abraham's earlier extravagant feast {things Abraham prepared}. There is a further irony in the language used in these two chapters if the latter set is the primary one. Abraham promised a "bite" and prepared fine cakes and an animal. Lot promises a feast but prepares only unleavened bread.[8]

---

[8] For a good discussion on the nature of Abraham's provisions there is Sarna, *JPS Torah Commentary: Genesis,* 129; and Wenham, *Genesis 26–50,* 11.

4a טֶרֶם יִשְׁכָּבוּ

4b וְאַנְשֵׁי הָעִיר אַנְשֵׁי סְדֹם נָסַבּוּ עַל־הַבַּיִת מִנַּעַר וְעַד־זָקֵן כָּל־הָעָם מִקָּצֶה:

4a Adv-V
4b **S-V-PP-Right-Dislocation (PP-PP-S-PP)**

Verse 4b introduces the "men of Sodom" for the first time. They cannot be fronted as a topic. There is no obvious contextual or logical set for the Sodomites to be contrasted with. Thus this represents a basic SV clause at the beginning of a new scene. The waw conjunction is considered a disjunctive waw and normally explained as signaling circumstantial information.

5a וַיִּקְרְאוּ אֶל־לוֹט וַיֹּאמְרוּ לוֹ

5b אַיֵּה הָאֲנָשִׁים

5c אֲשֶׁר־בָּאוּ אֵלֶיךָ הַלָּיְלָה

5d הוֹצִיאֵם אֵלֵינוּ

5e וְנֵדְעָה אֹתָם:

5a **V-PP-V-PP**
5b **Q-S**
5c   Rel-V-PP-AA
5d **V-PP**
5e **V-O**

6a וַיֵּצֵא אֲלֵהֶם לוֹט הַפֶּתְחָה

6b וְהַדֶּלֶת סָגַר אַחֲרָיו:

6a V-PP-S-AA
6b **O-V-PP**

In v. 6b the object has been fronted for focus. The contrast is between "the door" and "the doorway" from the previous line. Both belong to the logical set of {components of a home entrance}. The focus is on Lot's interaction with the entrance. He walks through the doorway, but he shuts the door.

"The door" is not thematic and cannot serve as a topic, unless the mention of "the entrance" activates "the door" on the basis of common knowledge. If such is the case, then it can be marked as a topic. The sense would be comparable to a left-dislocation in English, "He went out to them at the entrance. As for the door, he closed it behind him."

7a וַיֹּאמַר
7b אַל־נָא אַחַי תָּרֵעוּ׃

7a   **V**
7b   Neg-Voc-**V**

8a הִנֵּה־נָא לִי שְׁתֵּי בָנוֹת
8b אֲשֶׁר לֹא־יָדְעוּ אִישׁ

8a   Part-**Pred** (PP)-**S**
8b   Rel-**V-S**

8c אוֹצִיאָה־נָּא אֶתְהֶן אֲלֵיכֶם
8d וַעֲשׂוּ לָהֶן כַּטּוֹב בְּעֵינֵיכֶם

8c   **V-O**-PP
8d   **V**-PP-PP

8e רַק לָאֲנָשִׁים הָאֵל אַל־תַּעֲשׂוּ דָבָר
8f כִּי־עַל־כֵּן בָּאוּ בְּצֵל קֹרָתִי׃

8e   Part-PP-**V-O**
8f   Part-**V**-PP

9a וַיֹּאמְרוּ
9b גֶּשׁ־הָלְאָה

9a   **V**
9b   **V**-Adv

9c וַיֹּאמְרוּ
9d הָאֶחָד בָּא־
9e לָגוּר
9f וַיִּשְׁפֹּט שָׁפוֹט
9g עַתָּה נָרַע לְךָ מֵהֶם

9c   **V**
9d   <u>**S-V**</u>
9e   **V**(Inf)
9f   **V**
9g   Adv-**V**-PP-PP

The SV order in v. 9d marks the topic. "This one" (Lot) is an active theme in the minds of the speakers, as are the angelic visitors. "This one" is fronted to select Lot over the visitors as the new subject of the Sodomite's discourse moving forward.

9h וַיִּפְצְר֣וּ בָאִ֤ישׁ בְּלוֹט֙ מְאֹ֔ד
9i וַֽיִּגְּשׁ֖וּ לִשְׁבֹּ֥ר הַדָּֽלֶת׃

9h **V-O**-App-Adv
9i **V**-Compl (Inf-O)

10a וַיִּשְׁלְח֤וּ הָֽאֲנָשִׁים֙ אֶת־יָדָ֔ם
10b וַיָּבִ֧יאוּ אֶת־ל֛וֹט אֲלֵיהֶ֖ם הַבָּ֑יְתָה
10c וְאֶת־הַדֶּ֖לֶת סָגָֽרוּ׃

10a **V-S-O**
10b **V-O**-PP-AA
10c **O-V**

11a וְֽאֶת־הָאֲנָשִׁ֞ים אֲשֶׁר־פֶּ֣תַח הַבַּ֗יִת הִכּוּ֙ בַּסַּנְוֵרִ֔ים מִקָּטֹ֖ן וְעַד־גָּד֑וֹל
11b וַיִּלְא֖וּ לִמְצֹ֥א הַפָּֽתַח׃

11a **O** (O-Rel-AA) **V**-PP-PP-PP
11b **V**-Compl (Inf-O)

The long object in v. 11a has been fronted as a topic. Among the numerous possible themes at this point in the discourse, "the men who were at the door" were selected to make explicit who was being struck blind.

12a וַיֹּאמְר֨וּ הָאֲנָשִׁ֜ים אֶל־ל֗וֹט
12b עֹ֚ד מִֽי־לְךָ֣ פֹ֔ה
12c חָתָן֙ וּבָנֶ֣יךָ וּבְנֹתֶ֔יךָ וְכֹ֥ל אֲשֶׁר־לְךָ֖ בָּעִ֑יר הוֹצֵ֖א מִן־הַמָּקֽוֹם׃
13a כִּֽי־מַשְׁחִתִ֣ים אֲנַ֔חְנוּ אֶת־הַמָּק֖וֹם הַזֶּ֑ה
13b כִּֽי־גָֽדְלָ֤ה צַעֲקָתָם֙ אֶת־פְּנֵ֣י יְהֹוָ֔ה
13c וַיְשַׁלְּחֵ֥נוּ יְהֹוָ֖ה לְשַׁחֲתָֽהּ׃

12a **V-S**-PP
12b Adv-Q-PP-Adv
12c **O-V**-PP
13a Part-**V**(ptcpl)-**S-O**
13b Part-**V-S**-PP
13c **V**(V-O)-**S**-Comp [Inf (Inf-O)]

Verse 12c has a fronted object. It is unclear whether the object should be considered to have a topic or focus marking. Focusing is more likely, but the intended contrast is not contextually clear.

14a וַיֵּצֵא לוֹט
14b וַיְדַבֵּר׀ אֶל־חֲתָנָיו
14c   לֹקְחֵי בְנֹתָיו
14d וַיֹּאמֶר֙

14a **V-S**
14b **V-PP**
14c   **V(ptcpl)-O**
14d **V**

14e קוּמוּ צְּאוּ מִן־הַמָּקוֹם הַזֶּה
14f   כִּי־מַשְׁחִית יְהוָה אֶת־הָעִיר
14g וַיְהִי כִמְצַחֵק בְּעֵינֵי חֲתָנָיו:

14e **V-V-PP**
14f   **Part-V(ptcpl)-S-O**
14g **V-PP-PP**

15a וּכְמוֹ֙ הַשַּׁחַר עָלָה
15b וַיָּאִיצוּ הַמַּלְאָכִים בְּלוֹט לֵאמֹר

15a <u>Prep-**S-V**</u>
15b **V-S-O**

Verse 15a is a case of subject fronting. I would expect that כְמוֹ would be a syntactic item triggering inversion. In which case, there should be VS order. However, the "dawn" has been fronted. This fronting is difficult to explain. It is unlikely that the dawn is being contrasted with anything and thus not in focus. It is not a discourse dependent theme, though it is arguably a theme since it can be assumed that all readers would have knowledge of "the dawn."[9] The best explanation available is that "the dawn" is selected as topic over other possible themes such as "Lot" and "his sons-in-law."

---

[9] So Holmstedt concludes with adverbial particles like "yesterday" ("Word Order and Information Structure," 128).

15c קוּם֩ קַ֨ח אֶת־אִשְׁתְּךָ֜ וְאֶת־שְׁתֵּ֤י בְנֹתֶ֙יךָ֙

15d   הַנִּמְצָאֹ֔ת

15e   פֶּן־תִּסָּפֶ֖ה בַּעֲוֺ֥ן הָעִֽיר׃

15c   **V-V-O**

15d   Ptcpl

15e   Part-**V**-PP

16a וַֽיִּתְמַהְמָ֓הּ

16b וַיַּחֲזִ֨קוּ הָאֲנָשִׁ֜ים בְּיָד֣וֹ וּבְיַד־אִשְׁתּ֗וֹ וּבְיַד֙ שְׁתֵּ֣י בְנֹתָ֔יו בְּחֶמְלַ֥ת יְהוָ֖ה עָלָ֑יו

16c וַיֹּצִאֻ֥הוּ

16d וַיַּנִּחֻ֖הוּ מִח֥וּץ לָעִֽיר׃

16a   **V**

16b   **V-S-O**-PP

16c   **V**(V-O)

16d   **V**(V-O)-PP

17a וַיְהִ֞י כְהוֹצִיאָ֤ם אֹתָם֙ הַח֔וּצָה

17b וַיֹּ֙אמֶר֙

17a   TempP(**V**-PP-**O**-AA)

17b   **V**

17c הִמָּלֵ֖ט עַל־נַפְשֶׁ֑ךָ

17d אַל־תַּבִּ֣יט אַחֲרֶ֔יךָ

17e וְאַֽל־תַּעֲמֹ֖ד בְּכָל־הַכִּכָּ֑ר הָהָ֛רָה

17f הִמָּלֵ֖ט

17g פֶּן־תִּסָּפֶֽה׃

17c   **V**-PP

17d   **V**-PP

17e   **V**-PP-AA

17f   **V**

17g   Part-**V**

18a וַיֹּ֥אמֶר ל֖וֹט אֲלֵהֶ֑ם

18b אַל־נָ֖א אֲדֹנָֽי׃

18a   **V-S**-PP

18b   Neg-Voc

19a הֲנֵה־נָא מָצָא עַבְדְּךָ חֵן בְּעֵינֶיךָ
19b וַתַּגְדֵּל חַסְדְּךָ
19c אֲשֶׁר עָשִׂיתָ עִמָּדִי
19d לְהַחֲיוֹת אֶת־נַפְשִׁי

19a	Part-**V-S-O**-PP
19b	**V-O**
19c	Rel-V-PP
19d	**V**(Inf)-**S**

הִנֵּה does not cause triggered inversion.[10] The verb "he found" in v. 19a has been fronted. It is possible that this is a case of modality resulting in the VS order. Most translations go with an indicative sense and translate the clause something like, "Surely your servant has found favor in your eyes..." However, this can be seen as the initial line of Lot's request which follows in vv. 19b–20e. In this case, Lot asks from the beginning, "May your servant find favor in your eyes... please let me escape to this city."

19e וְאָנֹכִי לֹא אוּכַל לְהִמָּלֵט הָהָרָה
19f פֶּן־תִּדְבָּקַנִי הָרָעָה
19g וָמַתִּי

19e	**S-V**-Comp (Inf-AA)
19f	Part-**V**(V-O)-**S**
19g	**V**

Verse 19e is a case of a focused constituent. The inclusion of the pronoun points away from this being understood as a basic clause. Lot is contrasting himself with members of the logical set {ones who travel to the mountains}.

20a הִנֵּה־נָא הָעִיר הַזֹּאת קְרֹבָה לָנוּס שָׁמָּה
20b וְהִיא מִצְעָר

20a	Part-**S-Pred**(Adj-Inf-Adv)
20b	**S-Pred**

---

[10] Holmstedt, "Word Order and Information Structure," 131.

אִמְלְטָה נָּא שָׁמָּה 20c
הֲלֹא מִצְעָר הִוא 20d
וּתְחִי נַפְשִׁי: 20e

20c   V-Adv
20d   **Q-Pred-S**
20e   **V-S**

וַיֹּאמֶר אֵלָיו 21a
הִנֵּה נָשָׂאתִי פָנֶיךָ 21b
גַּם לַדָּבָר הַזֶּה 21c
לְבִלְתִּי הָפְכִּי אֶת־הָעִיר 21d
אֲשֶׁר דִּבַּרְתָּ: 21e

21a   **V-PP**
21b   Part-**V-O**
21c   Part-PP
21d   InfP(Neg-Inf-Subj)-**O**
21e   Rel-**V**

מַהֵר הִמָּלֵט שָׁמָּה 22a
כִּי לֹא אוּכַל לַעֲשׂוֹת דָּבָר עַד־בֹּאֲךָ שָׁמָּה 22b
עַל־כֵּן קָרָא שֵׁם־הָעִיר צוֹעַר: 22c

22a   **V-V**-Adv
22b   Part-**V**-Comp(Inf-**O**)-PP
22c   Part-**V-O-O**

הַשֶּׁמֶשׁ יָצָא עַל־הָאָרֶץ 23a
וְלוֹט בָּא צֹעֲרָה: 23b
וַיהֹוָה הִמְטִיר עַל־סְדֹם וְעַל־עֲמֹרָה גָּפְרִית וָאֵשׁ מֵאֵת יְהֹוָה מִן־הַשָּׁמָיִם: 24

23a   **S-V-PP**
23b   **S-V-AA**
24   **S-V-PP-O-PP-PP**

Each subject in the three lines of vv. 23a–24 are fronted as topics. "The sun" is a non-contextually defined theme—we can assume all readers have knowledge of the sun. In each successive line a new topic is switched to abruptly and each is marked with fronting in order to facilitate this.

25 וַיַּהֲפֹךְ אֶת־הֶעָרִים הָאֵל וְאֵת כָּל־הַכִּכָּר וְאֵת כָּל־יֹשְׁבֵי הֶעָרִים וְצֶמַח הָאֲדָמָה:

25   **V-O**

26a וַתַּבֵּט אִשְׁתּוֹ מֵאַחֲרָיו
26b וַתְּהִי נְצִיב מֶלַח:

26a   **V-S-PP**
26b   **V-Pred**

27a וַיַּשְׁכֵּם אַבְרָהָם בַּבֹּקֶר אֶל־הַמָּקוֹם
27b   אֲשֶׁר־עָמַד שָׁם אֶת־פְּנֵי יְהוָה:

27a   V-S-PP-PP
27b   Rel-V-Adv-PP

28a וַיַּשְׁקֵף עַל־פְּנֵי סְדֹם וַעֲמֹרָה וְעַל־כָּל־פְּנֵי אֶרֶץ הַכִּכָּר
28b וַיַּרְא
28c וְהִנֵּה עָלָה קִיטֹר הָאָרֶץ כְּקִיטֹר הַכִּבְשָׁן:

28a   **V-PP**
28b   **V**
28c   <u>Part-**V**-**S**-PP-PP</u>

This clause exhibits a fronted verb. הִנֵּה is not a syntactic trigger of inversion.[11] We expect SV order here. An irreal understanding makes no sense in context. The verb as a topic is equally non-sensical. Therefore, the verb has been focus fronted. The reason for the focus is not clear.

29a וַיְהִי בְּשַׁחֵת אֱלֹהִים אֶת־עָרֵי הַכִּכָּר
29b וַיִּזְכֹּר אֱלֹהִים אֶת־אַבְרָהָם

29a   TempP[**V**-PP(Prep-Inf-**S**-**O**)]
29b   **V**-**S**-**O**

29c וַיְשַׁלַּח אֶת־לוֹט מִתּוֹךְ הַהֲפֵכָה
29d בַּהֲפֹךְ אֶת־הֶעָרִים
29e   אֲשֶׁר־יָשַׁב בָּהֵן לוֹט:

29c   **V**-**O**-PP
29d   TempP (Prep-Inf-**O**)
29e   Rel-**V**-PP-**S**

---

[11] Holmstedt, "Word Order and Information Structure," 131.

וַיַּעַל לֹוט מִצֹּועַר 30a

30a   **V-S-PP**

וַיֵּשֶׁב בָּהָר 30b
וּשְׁתֵּי בְנֹתָיו עִמֹּו 30c
כִּי יָרֵא לָשֶׁבֶת בְּצֹועַר 30d

30b   **V-PP**
30c   **S-Pred**(PP)
30d   Part-**V**-Comp(Inf-PP)

וַיֵּשֶׁב בַּמְּעָרָה הוּא וּשְׁתֵּי בְנֹתָיו: 30e
30e   **V-PP**-Right Dislocation

וַתֹּאמֶר הַבְּכִירָה אֶל־הַצְּעִירָה 31a
31a   **V-S-PP**

אָבִינוּ זָקֵן 31b
וְאִישׁ אֵין בָּאָרֶץ לָבֹוא עָלֵינוּ כְּדֶרֶךְ כָּל־הָאָרֶץ: 31c
31b   **S-Pred**
31c   **S-Pred** (Part-PP)-Comp (Inf-PP-PP)

Whether זָקֵן is taken as a verb or an adjective, v. 31b would be
considered basic word order. There is no reason to focus "our father"
and though Lot is an active discourse theme, he is not a theme at the
level of the two sisters' conversation. This is a basic clause at the beginning of their interaction.

לְכָה נַשְׁקֶה אֶת־אָבִינוּ יַיִן 32a
וְנִשְׁכְּבָה עִמֹּו 32b
וּנְחַיֶּה מֵאָבִינוּ זָרַע: 32c

32a   **V-V-O-O**
32b   **V-PP**
32c   **V-PP-O**

וַתַּשְׁקֶיןָ אֶת־אֲבִיהֶן יַיִן בַּלַּיְלָה הוּא 33a
וַתָּבֹא הַבְּכִירָה 33b
וַתִּשְׁכַּב אֶת־אָבִיהָ 33c
וְלֹא־יָדַע בְּשִׁכְבָהּ וּבְקוּמָהּ: 33d

33a   **V-O-O**-PP
33b   **V-S**
33c   **V**-PP
33d   **V**-Compl (PP-PP)

34a וַיְהִי֙ מִֽמָּחֳרָ֔ת
34b וַתֹּ֤אמֶר הַבְּכִירָה֙ אֶל־הַצְּעִירָ֔ה

34a   TempP(**V**-PP)
34b   **V-S**-PP

34c הֵן־שָׁכַ֥בְתִּי אֶ֖מֶשׁ אֶת־אָבִ֑י
34d נַשְׁקֶ֨נּוּ יַ֜יִן גַּם־הַלַּ֗יְלָה

34c   Part-**V**-Adv-PP
34d   **V-O**-Adv

34e וּבֹ֙אִי֙ שִׁכְבִ֣י עִמּ֔וֹ
34f וּנְחַיֶּ֥ה מֵאָבִ֖ינוּ זָֽרַע׃

34e   **V-V**-PP
34f   **V**-PP-**O**

35a וַתַּשְׁקֶ֜יןָ גַּ֣ם בַּלַּ֧יְלָה הַה֛וּא אֶת־אֲבִיהֶ֖ן יָ֑יִן
35b וַתָּ֤קָם הַצְּעִירָה֙
35c וַתִּשְׁכַּ֣ב עִמּ֔וֹ
35d וְלֹֽא־יָדַ֥ע בְּשִׁכְבָ֖הּ וּבְקֻמָֽהּ׃

35a   **V**-Adv-**O-O**
35b   **V-S**
35c   **V**-PP
35d   **V**-Comp (PP-PP)

36a וַֽתַּהֲרֶ֛יןָ שְׁתֵּ֥י בְנֽוֹת־ל֖וֹט מֵאֲבִיהֶֽן׃

36a   **V-S**-PP

37a וַתֵּ֤לֶד הַבְּכִירָה֙ בֵּ֔ן
37b וַתִּקְרָ֥א שְׁמ֖וֹ מוֹאָ֑ב

37a   **V-S-O**
37b   **V-O-O**

37c ה֥וּא אֲבִֽי־מוֹאָ֖ב עַד־הַיּֽוֹם׃

37c   **S-Pred**-PP

38a וְהַצְּעִירָה גַם־הִוא֙ יָלְדָה בֵּ֑ן
38b וַתִּקְרָא שְׁמ֖וֹ בֶּן־עַמִּ֑י
38c ה֣וּא אֲבִ֥י בְנֵֽי־עַמּ֖וֹן עַד־הַיּֽוֹם: ס

38a   S-Adv-**V-O**
38b   **V-O-O**
38c   **S-Pred**-PP

The SV order of v. 38a is expected. However, the subject is fronted for focus. The younger sister is being contrasted/compared with her older sister, this is reinforced גַם־הִוא.

6.3. *Summary*

Thirty-two clauses with order that depart from basic SVO for either pragmatic or semantic reasons have been found in the Sodom episode. Seven of these are for the semantic reason of distinguishing irreal from indicative verbs. Eleven of these clauses either exhibit what is expected for basic order or lack an explicit subject. Those that lack an explicit subject are irreal verbs that are raised over a null subject. Those that exhibit the expected basic SV order, but are still said to have pragmatic marking are understood in such terms purely from context. Holmstedt's information structure subordinates the standard discourse functions applied to SV order (circumstantial comments, new scene opening) to pragmatic marking as far as the rationale for the SV word order. Fronted word order marks items pragmatically, and clauses with certain items marked pragmatically are naturally suitable for certain discourse functions. Other discourse functions are more free (e.g., beginning a new episode with new characters) and basic word order can occur. Word order itself does not technically signal a discourse function, though it still functions as a diagnostic of those discourse functions.

Chapter 7
CONCLUSIONS

Upon examining the data, there are relatively few differences in semantic and pragmatic meaning between the two views. This is even taking into account syntactic triggers of inversion in the SVO view. The main causes of the unexpectedly small number of differences are the clauses that I have called implicitly marked. Holmstedt sees clauses that would otherwise be considered to have a basic surface order, as still potentially exhibiting topic and/or focus marking. After taking this into account, there are not any major noticeable trends that differentiate the two views over the course of the Sodom episode. When the narrative participants and characters are tracked over the course of the story, and a list is made of which characters receive fronting, the two views produce almost identical lists.[1]

The differences that are observed provide the answer to my initial research question: "What is the practical relationship between one's view of Biblical Hebrew's basic word order and the semantic interpretation of clauses in classical Hebrew prose as exemplified in Gen 18–19?" The answer is that in Gen 18–19 an interpreter's view of BH's word order affects the semantic-pragmatic interpretation of non-consecutive verb first and subject first clauses with no other fronted elements. The SVO view requires such verb first clauses to be understood as conveying non-indicative mood or with a pragmatic

---

[1] From the VSO point of view a sequential list of fronted characters: My lord (Abraham), I (Sarah), Sarah, YHWH, Abraham, The judge of all the earth (YHWH), Abraham, The men of the city, This one (Lot), The men of the city, Lot's family, The dawn, I (Lot), The Sun, Lot, YHWH, and The Younger Sister. From the SVO point of view a sequential list of fronted characters: I(Sarah), Sarah, YHWH, Abraham, Abraham, The Judge of all the earth (YHWH), Abraham, This one (YHWH), The men of the city, Lot's family, The dawn, Lot, The Sun, Lot, YHWH, The Younger Sister

marking on the verb. The VSO view understands such verb first clauses to be basic and they are to be interpreted indicatively and without
any special emphasis. The VSO view requires that subject first clauses
with no other fronted elements be understood as having a pragmatic
marking. The SVO view allows such clauses to be understood as basic,
with no special emphasis.

7.1. Markedness in the Sodom Episode Summarized

In the following tables I have tallied the marked clauses from
Gen 18–19 from both points of view so that they can be quickly compared. Table 1 shows all the clauses that are considered marked from
the VSO perspective. Table 2 shows the clauses that are considered
marked only from the VSO perspective. The data from the SVO position has been split into two types of marking. From Holmstedt's generative approach, there can be SV clauses that exhibit a surface order
identical to the basic order, but nonetheless are considered to have
fronted/marked constituents. I have called such clauses implicitly
marked. Explicitly marked clauses are those that exhibit a word order
that departs from basic word order. Table 3 shows all explicitly
marked clauses from the SVO perspective. Table 4 shows all clauses
that are only considered marked from the SVO perspective. Table 5
shows all implicitly marked clauses from the SVO perspective. Table
6 shows all implicitly marked clauses that are only considered marked
from the SVO perspective.

Table 1: VSO MARKED CLAUSES

18:7a	19:2i	19:23a
18:12c	19:3e	19:23b
18:13d	19:4b	19:24
18:14b	19:6b	19:38a
18:14c	19:9d	
18:17a	19:10c	

18:17b	19:11a	
18:18a	19:12c	
18:25d	19:15a	
18:33c	19:19c	24 Total

Table 2: UNIQUE VSO MARKED CLAUSES

| 18:12c | 19:4b | 2 Total |

Table 3: SVO EXPLICITLY MARKED CLAUSES

18:4a	19:2f	19:28c
18:7a	19:2i	
18:11c	19:3e	
18:14b	19:6b	
18:14c	19:10c	
18:17b	19:11a	
18:18b	19:12c	
18:25d	19:15a	
18:26c	19:19a	
19:2e	19:19c	21 Total

Table 4: UNIQUE SVO EXPLICITLY MARKED CLAUSES

18:4a	18:26c	19:19a
18:11c	19:2e	19:28c
18:18b	19:2f	
		8 Total

Table 5: SVO IMPLICITLY MARKED CLAUSES

18:13d	18:22c	19:23b
18:17a	18:33c	19:24
18:18a	19:9d	19:38a
18:19c	19:23a	

11 Total

Table 6: UNIQUE SVO IMPLICITLY MARKED CLAUSES

18:19c	18:22c	2 Total

7.2. Examining the Differences

The clauses that remain with noticeable difference in interpretation are 18:12c, 19:4b, 18:11c, 19:19a, and 19:28c. Of these, only two can be said to potentially affect the exegesis of the passage: 18:11c and 19:19a. The nature of the interpretational differences between the clauses and their relationship to the exegesis of Gen 18–19 will be discussed below.

7.2.1. Irreal Verbs

The majority of unique clauses that depart from the basic order in the SVO view are a result of viewing the basic word order of irreal clauses to be VS. From an SVO view, the VS order of a clause such as 18:18b is not translated with a contingent future value simply by virtue of being a *weqatal*. The verb first order of the *weqatal* is explained as being the result of the verb form being an irreal *qatal*. Clauses that do not feature *weqatals* but contain a *yiqtol* (such as 18:4a) are also taken as irreal by their VS order. 18:4a does include the particle נָא, which informs the reader to take the *yiqtol* as a jussive. However, from the

SVO point of view, the word order is a further, if not the more prima-ry, signal of the jussive.

The interpretation of most of the irreal clauses in the sample corpus does not differ between the two views. Though the SVO framework requires that these clauses be interpreted as irreal, the VSO framework would also understand these clauses to be irreal,[2] but not indicated so by word order. The real difference between the two views arises in cases where the modality of a verb is in question or open for debate.

Word order could potentially serve to aid the reader in deciding between an irreal and indicative interpretation in the case of ambiguous *yiqtol* forms (i.e., those whose short and long form are identical and have no accompanying modal particles in context). Furthermore, it might be found that word order signals irreal sense for *qatal* verbs apart from the *weqatal* form or signaling particles.[3]

The one example of such a case in Gen 18–19 would be 19:19a.

19:19a הִנֵּה־נָא מָצָא עַבְדְּךָ חֵן בְּעֵינֶיךָ

The traditional way to translate מָצָא in this verse is with an indicative value. The KJV, ESV, NASB, NIV, NLT, and HCSB all give a simple past tense here. "See, your servant found favor in your eyes." However, because there is no syntactic trigger that would cause

---

[2] There is disagreement over whether *weqatal* should be considered a mod-al form, however the translation values given are the same.

[3] It is undisputed that there are irreal uses of *qatal* forms, such as when a *qatal* form follows a particle like אִם. This is one of the weaknesses of the morpho-logical designations of verb forms. Many *qatal* verbs would naturally be considered the same as a *weqatal* if the real-irreal binary is being employed. See Cook, "Recon-sidering," 11–13. This builds on Revell's initial observations but departs from his conclusion that distinguished between the *qatal* and *weqatal* by taking the latter as a way of marking an indicative imperfect. See Revell, "System," 32–33. Eric J. Tully applies the word order criteria for identifying irreal *qatal* verbs in *Hosea: A Hand-book on the Hebrew Text*, Baylor Handbook on the Hebrew Bible (Waco, TX: Baylor University Press, Forthcoming).

the VS order, מָצָא must either be fronted for a pragmatic reason, or be
an irreal verb. In this case the context favors the irreal interpretation.
This clause could be translated with an optative value as the beginning
of Lot's request to be allowed to escape to the "small town" of Zoar.
"Please, may your servant find favor in your eyes." This is a reading
not generally recognized as a possibility by the traditional VSO approach.[4]

Such a reading potentially adds evidence to seeing an inten-
tionally negative portrayal of Lot.[5] The angelic visitors have essentially manhandled Lot out of the city. They have gone to great lengths
to make sure that he and his family would be spared when Sodom and
Gomorrah receive judgment from heaven. Instead of recognizing and
thanking the visitors for their many acts of kindness, Lot asks for favor
as if he has not received any yet. While potentially an act of humility,
this could also be taken as ungrateful. Furthermore, 19:29 summarizes
the episode as God "remembering Abraham" in the midst of His de-
structive judgment. An ungrateful Lot at this point would reinforce
that his fortunes have been the result of God's faithfulness to Abraham, and not his own merit.

7.2.2. Simple SVO Clauses Without a Fronted Constituent

Every case of fronting that is unique to the VSO view (18:12c,
19:4b, 19:19e) is the result of understanding that an SVO clause must
be marked in some sense. The reason that there are not more unique
examples is that Holmstedt's SVO view includes the concepts of triggered inversion (X-SVO is the marked order) and implicitly marked

---

[4] This understanding could account for the times when JM records that the
qatal "sometimes seems to have an optative nuance" (112.K, 336–37).

[5] George W. Coats gives a fuller literary account of a negative portrayal for
Lot in "Lot: A Foil in the Abraham Saga," in *Understanding the Word: Essays in
Honor of Bernhard W. Anderson* ed. James T. Butler, Edgar W. Conrad, and Ben C.
Ollenburger (Sheffield: JSOT Press, 1985), 113–32. Paul Tonson provides an op-
posing take, "Mercy Without Covenant: A Literary Analysis of Genesis 19," *JSOT*
95 (2001): 95–116.

SVO clauses. There is much overlap between the two views concerning which clauses are considered marked.

18:12c וַאדֹנִי זָקֵן:

19:4b וְאַנְשֵׁי הָעִיר אַנְשֵׁי סְדֹם נָסַבּוּ עַל־הַבַּיִת מִנַּעַר וְעַד־זָקֵן כָּל־הָעָם מִקָּצֶה:

It is interesting to note that neither of these clauses feature an unequivocally marked topic or focus in either view. Both 18:12c and 19:4b are considered as marking the clause as a whole by VSO proponents. The pragmatic status of the subject in these cases is not different between the SVO and VSO views. The question is whether or not these clauses are marked as performing a discourse function by the word order.

It is clear that in context, one can accurately describe these clauses and other similar ones with the functions that have been assigned to them by VSO proponents (e.g., starting a new episode, switching scenes, providing justification, etc). The obvious question is whether such functions are signaled by variation from the basic word order, or known by context and open to employing a basic word order. One way to begin to answer this question would be a cross-linguistic study of literature in other languages. Such study should be done to determine whether or not the discourse functions attributed to marked word order by VSO proponents are performed by marked structures or unmarked structures in other languages. If it can be determined that the same structures used to mark topic and focus are employed for clause-level functions in other languages, this would provide cross-linguistic support to the VSO position.[6]

7.2.3. Simple VSO Clauses Without a Fronted Constituent
There are two clauses that require a marked interpretation that

---

[6] The converse is also obviously true. If it proves that topic and focus structures are not usually used for clause-level functions in other languages, then this would argue against VSO program.

are unique to the SVO view—18:11c and 19:28c. These types of
clauses provide even more fruitful ground for examining differences in
exegetical consequences than do the simple SVO clauses of the previous section. Of the two clauses in Gen 18–19, 18:11c proves to be the
most exegetically significant.

18:11c חָדַל לִהְיוֹת לְשָׂרָה אֹרַח כַּנָּשִׁים:

Understanding the verb as marked in 18:11c makes a great deal
of sense contextually. If the verb has been focused, then a number of
possible effects are produced. The miraculous nature of Isaac's birth is
linguistically signaled as central to the storyline. More immediately,
Sarah's incredulity is meant to be shared momentarily by the audience.
Readers are to feel the same surprise because the narrator wants them
to focus on the fact that "the way of women had stopped for Sarah."
Sarah's inability to have children is not a parenthetical comment meant
to let readers know that the conception would be miraculous. Sarah's
physical state takes a central place in grammar of the verse and surrounding verses as the most salient piece of information relative to the
current events.

The difference can be illustrated if one imagines the narrator
addressing the audience with the information contained in this clause.
If this is a basic VSO clause one would render the sense as a simple
circumstantial statement, "And by the way, Sarah was past menopause." David Cotter describes this clause as a brief intrusion to in-
form or remind (given Abraham's earlier statement of age in Gen
17:17) the reader that Sarah was unable to have a child.[7] To use a theatre metaphor, this clause sets the stage for understanding what follows. However, if SVO is the basic order and the verb חָדַל has been
marked for focus, then one could render the sense, "Now listen to me,
Sarah *was past menopause!*" In the theatre metaphor, this clause takes

---

[7] David W. Cotter, *Genesis in Berit Olam: Studies in Hebrew Narrative &
Poetry* (Collegeville, MN: Liturgical Press, 2003), 118.

centerstage. Sarah is the first case of the "barren woman conceiving" motif. This type of event becomes a strong theme throughout the Old Testament. YHWH faithfully provides and overcomes physical limitations to see His promises through to the end. It makes sense that her inability to have children would be highlighted in the very grammar of the verse here.

The subjective effect of causing the readers to share in Sarah's disbelief can leave an important impression with the readers. God is able to do the surprising in order to fulfill His covenant promises. The first readers of Genesis and even most modern readers are aware of Sarah's inability to have children. Therefore, the promise and birth of Isaac can at times be brushed quickly over. A focus on Sarah's menopause would guide readers to focus on YHWH's ability to fulfill. By aiding the reader in sharing in Sarah's own disbelief for the moment, the narrator encourages the audience to have faith in the midst of bleak looking circumstances.

Apart from exegetical factors, VSO proponents need to give a satisfactory explanation of the structure of 18:11c. If חָדַל is not taken to be marked for focus, then for what reason is there an asyndetic clause? Why not a *wayyiqtol* or a disjunctive waw on אֹרַח to begin the clause? The clause shape is obviously unusual and one might further wonder why this is so in the Bible. Why are there not more simple VS clauses if VS is the standard order?

19:28c וְהִנֵּה עָלָה קִיטֹר הָאָרֶץ כְּקִיטֹר הַכִּבְשָׁן׃

A similarly satisfying explanation of the fronting of the verb is not immediately apparent for 19:28c. 19:28c proves itself to be a key verse for both sides. If understanding עָלָה as marked proves to be impossible and more such clauses can be produced in the Bible then the current SVO model would need revising.

Care must be taken not to press the exegetical musings in these conclusions too far. The readings, if they rest primarily on variation from a proposed basic word order, are weakly established. For example, the fact that it is significant that Sarah is barren can be ascertained apart from word order signaling. The exegetical insights are preliminary proposals in line with the proposed information structures. Ultimately, they must be supported by more than word order. I have attempted to show how one might interpret the word order variation by means of the context. Each information structure needs further testing in order to establish any proposed readings here.

7.3. Summary of Exegetical Observations

The view one adopts of basic word order in BH will not change the way one views the development of the Sodom narrative as a whole.[8] The key differences are to be found in the specific interpretation of isolated clauses. The nature of the types of clauses that present with these differences means that similar clauses in other contexts still have the potential to have wider-reaching exegetical ramifications. The most obvious ground for wider-reaching ramifications is the issue of word order and modality. In the Sodom episode, the clause with the potentially irreal verb (if SVO is adopted) in 19:19a would not be considered central to the interpretation of the narrative as a whole. However, the existence of such clauses in crucial areas is not hard to imagine. In New Testament studies the issue of the indicative vs subjunctive form of the verb ἔχω in Romans 5:1 comes to mind. Although the question in Romans 5:1 is one of textual variants, it still suffices as an example where the modality or indicative status of a verb in an indi-

---

[8] Sebastian Floor has attempted to move forward word order research by connecting word order and pragmatic structures to the identification of the theme of whole discourses (not 'theme' as in the linguistic term used in this work, but 'theme' as in the literary term). His work can be found in his introductory article Sebastiaan J. Floor, "From Word Order to Theme in Biblical Hebrew Narrative: Some Perspectives from Information Structure," *JSem* 12.2 (2003): 197–236; and also in the detailed treatment found in his dissertation, "From Information Structure, Topic and Focus, to Theme in Biblical Hebrew Narrative" (PhD thesis, The University of Stellenbosch, 2004); a proper understanding of word order and pragmatic function is crucial to further work like Floor's, unifying the linguistic and literary realms.

vidual clause has significant ramifications on the interpretation of the passage as a whole.

7.4. Conclusion and Suggestions for Further Research

It has been demonstrated that in a small but visible number of clauses that one's view on basic word order in BH constrains interpretation and will result in varying interpretations. These differences can be negligible but can also be potentially crucial to exegesis. The relevant clauses are simple SV and VS clauses without a fronted constituent and verb-first *yiqtol* and *qatal* clauses that might be irreal.

Because of their status as the clauses that produce the most differences between the two views, these clauses are also the most salient clauses for furthering the present word order debate. In these cases, one's word order view forces a pragmatic or semantic interpretation of a particular constituent. An in-context examination of clauses of the former type has the possibility to provide strong corroborating evidence for one's word-order view. The converse is also true, such clauses also provide the opportunity for a strong challenge to one's view. The pragmatic status of the first item in these types of clauses should be systematically studied. Ultimately it must be determined whether those cases wherein one is forced to see a pragmatic marking can be plausibly explained as adhering to their predetermined system. The next obvious step for the word order commentaries provided here would be to widen the corpus to all of Genesis and then eventually beyond.

Further study of clauses with irreal could include an examination of explicitly irreal verbs (by form, particle, or context) with an SV order for the purpose of determining whether or not the subject can be plausibly considered pragmatically marked in those instances. The SVO view needs to be able to account for SV clauses with irreal verbs. Furthermore, searches can be made for the types of clauses with potentially irreal verbs that are central to the interpretation of a passage, in order to assess the strengths and weaknesses of an irreal reading in those cases.

Additionally, there remains a question of larger discourse functions and their relationship to pragmatic marking. There can be two competing explanations for near-identical interpretations. Both camps predict for SVO order at the start of a new episode. So both camps might understand an individual SVO clause in the same way. However, the VSO camp argues that the word order is what specifically marks a clause as beginning an episode. The SVO camp argues that such a position in the narrative is the ideal place to find no pragmatic operators and one would expect basic order to appear.

An approach to answering this question using specifically BH data might be to pick a corpus and identify all clauses that perform a particular discourse level function (such as beginning a new episode) and study the word order of these clauses to see which word orders are most often employed (if any at all dominate) and work from there. Cross-linguistic evidence can be further adduced in the form of studies that examine the relationship between clauses that have relevant discourse level functions and the structures used to mark topic and focus in those same languages.

BIBLIOGRAPHY

Andersen, Francis I. *The Hebrew Verbless Clause in the Pentateuch*. Nashville: Abingdon, 1970.

_____. *The Sentence in Biblical Hebrew*. The Hague: Mouton, 1974.

Andersen, Henning. "Markedness Theory—The First 150 Years." Pages 11–46 in *Markedness in Synchrony and Diachrony*. Edited by Olga Miseska Tomic. Berlin: Mouton de Gruyter, 1989.

Arnold, Bill T. and John H. Choi. *A Guide to Biblical Hebrew Syntax*. New York: Cambridge University Press, 2003.

Bandstra, Barry L. "Word Order and Emphasis in Biblical Hebrew Narrative: Syntactic Observations on Genesis 22 from a Discourse Perspective." Pages 109–23 in *Linguistics and Biblical Hebrew*. Edited by Walter R. Bodine. Winona Lake, IN: Eisenbrauns, 1992.

Barr, James. *The Semantics of Biblical Language*. Oxford: Oxford University Press, 2000.

Beckman, John C. ed. *Williams' Hebrew Syntax, Third Edition*. 3rd ed. Toronto: University of Toronto, 2007.

Bloomfield, Leonard. *Language*. Chicago: University of Chicago Press, 1933.

Bodine, Walter R. "The Study of Linguistics and Biblical Hebrew." Pages 1–5 in *Linguistics and Biblical Hebrew*. Edited by Walter R. Bodine. Winona Lake, IN: Eisenbrauns, 1992.

Bornemann, Robert. *A Grammar of Biblical Hebrew*. Eugene, OR: Wipf & Stock, 2011.

Buth, Randall. "Functional Grammar, Hebrew and Aramaic: An Integrated, Textlinguistic Approach to Syntax." Pages 77–102 in *Discourse Analysis of Biblical Literature: What It Is and What It Offers*. Edited by W. R. Bodine. Atlanta: SBL Press, 1995.

_____. "Topic and Focus in Hebrew Poetry: Psalm 51." Pages 83–96 in *Language in Context: Essays for Robert E. Longacre*. Edited by S. J. J. Hwang and W. Merrifield. Dallas: SIL International, 1995.

_____. "Word Order in Aramaic from the Perspective of Functional Grammar and Discourse Analysis." PhD thesis, University of California, 1987.

_____. "Word Order in the Verbless Clause: A Generative-Functional Approach." Pages 79–108 in *The Verbless Clause in Biblical Hebrew: Linguistic Approaches*. Edited by Cynthia L. Miller. Winona Lake, IN: Eisenbrauns, 1999.

Bybee, Joan. "Main Clauses are Innovative, Subordinate Clauses are Conservative: Consequences for the Nature of Constructions." Pages 1–18 in *Complex Sentences in Grammar and Discourse: Essays in Honor of Sandra A. Thompson*. Edited by Joan Bybee and Michael Noonan. Amsterdam: Benjamins, 2002

Carnie, Andrew. *Syntax: A Generative Approach*. Oxford: Blackwell, 2007.

Chao, Yuen Ren. *A Grammar of Spoken Chinese*. Berkley: University of California Press, 1968.

Choi, Kyoungwon. *An Analysis of Subject-Before-Finite-Verb Clauses in the Book of Genesis Based on Traditional Grammarians*. Saarbrücken: VDM Verlag Dr. Müller, 2008.

Chomsky, Noam. *Syntactic Structures*. The Hague: Mouton, 1957.

Coats, George W. "Lot: A Foil in the Abraham Saga." Pages 113–32 in *Understanding the Word: Essays in Honor of Bernhard W Anderson*. Edited by James T. Butler, Edgar W. Conrad, and Ben C. Ollenburger. Sheffield: JSOT Press, 1985.

Comrie, Bernard. *Language Universals and Linguistic Typology*. Chicago: University of Chicago Press, 1989.

Cook, John A. "Reconsidering the So-called Vav-Consecutive." Paper presented at the Annual Meeting of the SBL. New Orleans, LA, 23 November 2009.

Cook, John A., and Robert D. Holmstedt. *Beginning Biblical Hebrew: A Grammar and Illustrated Reader*. Grand Rapids: Baker Academic, 2013.

Cotter, David W. *Genesis in Berit Olam: Studies in Hebrew Narrative & Poetry*. Collegeville, MN: Liturgical Press, 2003.

Cotterell, Peter and Max Turner. *Linguistics and Biblical Interpretation*. Downers Grove, IL: InterVarsity Press, 1989.

DeCaen, Vincent. "On the Placement and Interpretation of the Verb in Standard Biblical Hebrew Prose." PhD dissertation, University of Toronto, 1995.

Dik, Simon C. *Functional Grammar*. Dordrecht: Foris, 1981.

_____. *The Theory of Functional Grammar: Part I: The Structure of the Clause*. Dordrecht: Foris, 1989.

Dijk, Teun A. van. *Text and Context. Explorations in the Semantics and Pragmatics of Discourse*. London: Longman, 1982.

Dooley, Robert A. and Stephen H. Levinsohn. *Analyzing Discourse: A Manual of Basic Concepts*. Dallas: SIL International, 2001.

Doron, Edit. "VSO and Left-Conjunct Agreement: Biblical Hebrew vs. Modern Hebrew." Pages 75–95 in *The Syntax of Verb-Initial Languages*. Edited by Andrew Carnie and Eithne Guilfoyle. Oxford: Oxford University Press, 2000.

Doukhan, Jacques B. *Hebrew for Theologians: A Textbook for the Study of Biblical Hebrew in Relation to Hebrew Thinking* (Lanham, MD: University Press of America, 1993).

Downing Pamela. "Word Order in Discourse: By Way of Introduction." Pages 1–28 in *Word Order in Discourse*. Edited by Pamela Downing and Michael Noonan, 1–28. Amsterdam: Benjamins, 1995.

Dryer, Matthew S. "Frequency and Pragmatically Unmarked Word Order." Pages 105–35 in *Word Order in Discourse*. Edited by Pamela Downing and Michael Noonan. Amsterdam: Benjamins, 1995

_____. "Order of Subject, Object, and Verb." Pages 330–31 in *The World Atlas of Language Structures*. Edited by Martin Haspelmath, Matthew S. Dryer, David Gil, and Bernard Comrie. Oxford: Oxford University Press, 2005.

_____. "Word Order." Pages 61–131 in *Language Typology and Syntactic Description Volume 1: Clause Structure*. Edited by Timothy Shopen. Cambridge: Cambridge University Press, 2007.

Fariss, Sherry Lynn. "Word Order in Biblical Hebrew Poetry." PhD thesis, The University of Texas, 2003

Floor, Sebastiaan J. "From Word Order to Theme in Biblical Hebrew Narrative: Some Perspectives from Information Structure." *JSem* 12.2 (2003): 197–236.

_____. "From Information Structure, Topic and Focus, to Theme in Biblical Hebrew Narrative." PhD thesis, The University of Stellenbosch, 2004.

_____. "Poetic Fronting in a Wisdom Poetry Text: The Information Structure of Proverbs 7." *JNSL* 31.1 (2005): 23–58.

Fuller, Russell T., and Kyoungwon Choi. *Invitation to Biblical Hebrew: A Beginning Grammar*. Grand Rapids: Kregel Academic & Professional, 2006.

_____. *Invitation to Biblical Hebrew Syntax: An Intermediate Grammar*. Grand Rapids: Kregel, 2017.

Futato, Mark D. *Beginning Biblical Hebrew*. Winona Lake, IN: Eisenbrauns, 2003.

Garrett, Duane A., and Jason S. DeRouchie. *A Modern Grammar for Biblical Hebrew*. Nashville: B&H Academic, 2009.

Gee, James Paul. *An Introduction to Discourse Analysis: Theory and Method*. London: Routledge, 2011.

Gibson, J. C. L. ed. *Davidson's Hebrew Syntax*. Edinburgh: T&T Clark, 2000.

Givón, Talmy. "The Drift from VSO to SVO in Biblical Hebrew: The Pragmatics of Tense-Aspect." Pages 184–254 in *Mechanisms of Syntactic Change*. Edited by Charles N. Li, 184–254. Austin: University of Texas, 1977.

Goldfajin, T. *Word Order and Time in Biblical Hebrew Narrative*. Oxford: Oxford University Press, 1998.

Greenberg, Joseph H. *Language Universals with Special Reference to Feature Hierarchies*. The Hague: Mouton, 1966.

_____. "Some Universals of Grammar with Particular Reference to the Order of Meaningful Elements." Pages 73–113 in *Universals of Language*. Edited by Joseph Greenberg. Cambridge, MA: MIT, 1963.

Groom, Sue. *Linguistic Analysis of Biblical Hebrew*. Exeter: Paternoster, 2007.

Gross, Walter. "Is There Really a Compound Nominal Clause in Biblical Hebrew?" Pages 297–320 in *The Verbless Clause in Biblical Hebrew: Linguistic Approaches*. Edited by Cynthia L. Miller. Winona Lake, IN: Eisenbrauns, 1999.

Gundel, Jeanette K. "On Different Kinds of Focus." Pages 293–305 in *Focus: Linguistic, Cognitive, and Computational Perspectives*. Edited by Peter Bosch and Rob van der Sandt, 293–305. New York: Cambridge University, 1999.

Gundel, Jeanette K. and Thorstein Fretheim. "Topic and Focus." Pages 175–96 in *The Handbook of Pragmatics*. Edited by Laurence R. Horn and Gregory Ward. Oxford: Blackwell, 2004.

Hamilton, Victor P. *The Book of Genesis: Chapters 18–50*. Grand Rapids: Eerdmans, 1995.

Heimerdinger, Jean-Marc. *Topic, Focus and Foreground in Ancient Hebrew Narratives*. Sheffield: Sheffield Academic, 1999

Hoffer, Victoria, Bonnie Pedrotti Kittel, and Rebecca Abts Wright. *Biblical Hebrew: Text and Workbook*. New Haven: Yale University Press, 2004.

Hoftijzer, Jacob. "The Hebrew Verbless Clause in the Pentateuch." *VT* 23.4 (1973): 446–510.

Holmstedt, Robert D. "Adjusting Our Focus (Review of Katsuomi Shimasaki, Focus Structure in Biblical Hebrew: A Study of Word Order and Information Structure)." *HS* 44 (2003): 203–15.

——————. "Constituents at the Edge in Biblical Hebrew." *KUSATU* 17 (2014): 110–58.

——————. "Historical Linguistics and Biblical Hebrew." Pages 97–124 in *Diachrony in Biblical Hebrew*. Edited by Cynthia L. Miller-Naudé and Ziony Zevit. Winona Lake, IN: Eisenbrauns, 2012.

——————. "Investigating the Possible Verb-Subject to Subject-Verb Shift in Ancient Hebrew: Methodological First Steps." *KUSATU* 15 (2013): 3–31.

_____. "Review of *Word-Order Variation in Biblical Hebrew Poetry: Differentiating Pragmatics and Poetics* by Nicholas P. Lunn." *JSS* 54.1 (2009): 305–7.

_____. "The Relative Clause in Biblical Hebrew: A Linguistic Analysis." PhD diss., University of Wisconsin-Madison, 2002.

_____. "The Typological Classifications of the Hebrew of Genesis: Subject-Verb or Verb-Subject?" *JHebS* 11 (2011): 1–39.

_____. "Word Order and Information Structure in Ruth and Jonah: A Generative-Typological Analysis." *JSS* 54.1 (2009): 111–39.

_____. "Word Order in the Book of Proverbs." Pages 135–54 in *Seeking out the Wisdom of the Ancients: Essays Offered to Honor Michael V. Fox on the Occasion of His Sixty-Fifth Birthday*. Edited by R. L. Troxel, K. G. Friebel, and D. R. Magary. Winona Lake, IN: Eisenbrauns, 2005.

Hornkohl, Aaron. "The Pragmatics of the X+Verb Structure in the Hebrew of Genesis: The Linguistic Functions and Associated Effects and Meanings of Intra-Clausal Fronted Constituents," *Ethnorêma* 1 (2005): 35–122.

Hostetter, Edwin C. *An Elementary Grammar of Biblical Hebrew*. Sheffield: T&T Clark, 2000.

Huang, Yan. *Pragmatics: Oxford Textbooks in Linguistics*. Oxford: Oxford University Press, 2014.

Jakobson, Roman. "Structure of the Russian Verb." Pages 1–14 in *Russian and Slavic Grammar: Studies 1931–1981*. Edited by Linda R. Waugh and Morris Halle. New York: Mouton, 1984.

Jongeling, Karel. "On the VSO Character of Hebrew." Pages 103–111 in *Studies in Hebrew and Aramaic Syntax: Presented to Professor J. Hoftijzer on the Occasion of His Sixty-Fifth Birthday*. Edited by K. Jongeling, H. L. Murre-van den Berg and L. Van Rompey. Leiden: Brill, 1991.

Joüon, Paul, and T. Muraoka. *A Grammar of Biblical Hebrew*. Roma:

Gregorian & Biblical Press, 2011.

Kautzsch, E., ed. Gesenius' *Hebrew Grammar*, translated by A. E. Cowley. Oxford: Clarendon, 1910.

Kelly, Paige H., Terry L. Burden, and Timothy G. Crawford. *A Handbook to Biblical Hebrew: An Introductory Grammar*. Grand Rapids: Eerdmans, 1994.

Kempson, Ruth. "The Syntax/Pragmatics Interface." Pages 529–48 in *The Cambridge Handbook of Pragmatics*. Edited by Keith Allan and Kasia M. Jaszczolt. Cambridge: Cambridge University Press, 2012.

Kim, Dong-Hyuk. *Early Biblical Hebrew, Late Biblical Hebrew, and Linguistic Variability: A Sociolinguistic Evaluation of the Linguistic Dating of Biblical Texts*. Leiden: Brill, 2013.

Lambdin, Thomas O. *An Introduction to Biblical Hebrew*. New York: Schribner's Sons, 1971.

Lambrecht, Knud. *Information Structure and Sentence Form: Topic, Focus, and the Mental Representations of Discourse Referents*. Cambridge: Cambridge University Press, 1994.

LaPalombara, Lyda E. *An Introduction to Grammar: Traditional, Structural, and Transformational*. Cambridge, MA: Winthrop, 1976.

Levinson, Stephen C. *Pragmatics*. Cambridge: Cambridge University Press, 1987.

Levinsohn, Stephen H. "Unmarked and Marked Instances of Topicalization in Hebrew." Pages 21–33 in *Work Papers of the Summer Institute of Linguistics, University of North Dakota Sessions*. Edited by Robert A. Dooley and J. Albert Bickford. Dallas: SIL International, 1990.

Long, Gary A. *Grammatical Concepts 101 for Biblical Greek*. Peabody, MA: Hendrickson, 2006.

——————. *Grammatical Concepts 101 for Biblical Hebrew*. 2nd ed. Grand Rapids: Baker Academic, 2013.

Longacre, Robert E. "Analysis of Preverbal Nouns in Biblical Hebrew Narrative." *JoTT* 5 (1992): 208–24.

_____. "Left Shifts in Strongly VSO Languages." Pages 331–54 in *Word Order in Discourse*. Edited by Pamela Downing and Michael Noonan. Amsterdam: Benjamins, 1995.

_____. "Why We Need a Verbal Revolution in Linguistics." Pages 247–70 in *Fifth LACUS Forum*. Edited by Wolfgang Wolck and Paul L. Garvin. Columbia, SC: Hornbeam, 1979.

_____. "Some Hermeneutic Observations on Textlinguistics and Text Theory in the Humanities." Pages 169–83 in *Functional Approaches to Language, Culture, and Cognition: Papers in honor of Sydney M. Lamb*. Edited by David G. Lockwood, Peter H. Fries, and James E. Copeland. Amsterdam: Benjamins, 2000.

Lunn, Nicholas P. *Word-Order Variation in Biblical Hebrew Poetry: Differentiating Pragmatics and Poetics*. Exeter: Paternoster, 2006.

Macdonald, Richard Charles, "Grammatical Analysis of Various Biblical Hebrew Texts According to a Traditional Semitic Grammar." PhD diss., Southern Baptist Theological Seminary, 2014.

Mathesius, Vilem. *A Functional Analysis of Present Day English on a General Linguistic Basis*. Edited by Josef Vachek. The Hague: Mouton, 1975.

Merwe, Christo H. J. van der. "An Overview of Hebrew Narrative Syntax." Pages 1–20 in *Narrative Syntax and the Hebrew Bible: Papers of the Tilburg Conference 1996*. Edited by E. J. Van Wolde. Leiden: Brill, 1997.

_____. "Explaining Fronting in Biblical Hebrew." *JNSL* 25.2 (1999): 173–86.

_____. "The Function of Word Order in Old Hebrew—with Special Reference to Cases where a Syntagmeme Precedes a Verb in Joshua." *JNSL* 17 (1991): 129–44.

_____. "Towards a Better Understanding of Biblical Hebrew Word Order (Review of Walter Gross's Die Satzteilfolge im Verbal-satz alttestamentlicher Prosa)." *JNSL* 25.1 (1999): 277–300.

Merwe, Christo H. J. van der, and Eep Talstra. "Biblical Hebrew Word Order: The Interface of Information Structure and Formal Features." *ZAH* 15/16 (2002/2003): 68–107.

Merwe, Christo H. J. van der, Jackie A. Naudé, and Jan H. Kroeze. *Biblical Hebrew Reference Grammar*. Sheffield: T&T Clark, 1999.

Miller, Cynthia. "Pivotal Issues in Analyzing the Verbless Clause." Pages 3–17 in *The Verbless Clause in Biblical Hebrew: Linguistic Approaches*. Edited by Cynthia L. Miller. Winona Lake, IN: Eisenbrauns, 1999.

_____. ed. *The Verbless Clause in Biblical Hebrew: Linguistic Approaches*. Winona Lake, IN: Eisenbrauns, 1999.

Miller-Naudé, Cynthia and Ziony Zevit, eds. *Diachrony in Biblical Hebrew*. Winona Lake, IN: Eisenbrauns, 2012.

Morris, C. W. "Foundations of the Theory of Signs" Pages 77–138 in *International Encyclopedia of Unified Science*. Edited by O.Neurath, R. Carnap, and C. Morris. Chicago: University of Chicago Press, 1938.

Moshavi, Adina. "The Discourse Functions of Object/Adverbial-Fronting in Biblical Hebrew." Pages 231–45 in *Biblical Hebrew in its Northwest Semitic Setting: Typological and Historical Perspectives*. Edited by Steven E. Fassberg and Avi Hurvitz. Winona Lake, IN: Eisenbrauns, 2006.

_____. "The Pragmatics of Word Order in Biblical Hebrew: A Statistical Analysis." PhD thesis, Yeshiva University, 2000.

_____. *Word Order in the Biblical Hebrew Finite Clause*. Winona Lake, IN: Eisenbrauns, 2010.

Muraoka, Takamitsu. *Emphatic Words and Structures in Biblical Hebrew*. Jerusalem: Magnes, 1985.

Niccacci, Alviero. *The Syntax of the Verb in Classical Hebrew Prose*. Sheffield: T&T Clark, 2009.

Payne, Doris L. ed. *Pragmatics of Word Order Flexibility*. Amsterdam: Benjamins, 1992.

Poythress, Vern S. *In the Beginning Was the Word: Language—A*

God-Centered Approach. Wheaton, IL: Crossway, 2009.

Pratico, Gary D., and Miles V. Van Pelt. *Basics of Biblical Hebrew Grammar: Second Edition*. Grand Rapids: Zondervan, 2014.

Prince, Ellen. "Topicalization and Left-Dislocation: A Functional Analysis." Pages 213–25 in *Discourses in Reading and Linguistics*. Edited by S. J. White and V. Teller. New York: New York Academy of Sciences, 1984.

_____. "Fancy Syntax and Shared Knowledge." *J.Pragmat* 9 (1985): 65–81.

_____. "On the Limits of Syntax, with Reference to Left-Dislocation and Topicalization." Pages 281–302 in *The Limits of Syntax*. Edited by Peter Culicover and Louise McNally. Leiden: Brill, 1988.

Regt, Lénart J. de. "The Order of Participants in Compound Clausal Elements in the Pentateuch and Earlier Prophets: Syntax, Convention or Rhetoric?" Pages 79–100 in *Literary Structure and Rhetorical Strategies in the Hebrew Bible*. Edited by L. J. D. Regt, J. D. Waard, and J. P. Fokkelman, 79–100. Winona Lake, IN: Eisenbrauns, 1996.

_____. "Macrosyntactic Functions of Nominal Clauses Referring to Participants." Pages 286–96 in *The Verbless Clause in Biblical Hebrew: Linguistic Approaches*. Edited by Cynthia L. Miller. Winona Lake, IN: Eisenbrauns, 1999.

_____. "Word Order in Different Clause Types in Deuteronomy 1–30." Pages 152–72 in *Studies in Hebrew and Aramaic Syntax Presented to Professor J. Hoftijzer on the Occasion of His Sixty-Fifth Birthday*. Edited by K. Jongeling, H. L. Murre-Van Den Berg and L. Van Rompay. Leiden: Brill, 1991.

Revell, E. J. "The Conditioning of Word Order in Verbless Clauses in Biblical Hebrew." *JSS* 34.1 (1989): 1–24.

_____. "The System of the Verb in Standard Biblical Prose." *HUCA* 60 (1989): 1–37.

_____. "Thematic Continuity and the Conditioning of Word Order in Verbless Clauses." Pages 297–320 in *The Verbless Clause in*

Biblical Hebrew: Linguistic Approaches. Edited by Cynthia L. Miller. Winona Lake, IN: Eisenbrauns, 1999.

Rosenbaum, Michael. *Word-Order Variation in Isaiah 40–55*. Assen: Van Gorcum, 1997.

Ross, Allen P. *Introducing Biblical Hebrew*. Grand Rapids: Baker Academic, 2001.

Sarna, Nahum M. *The JPS Torah Commentary: Genesis*. Philadelphia: The Jewish Publication Society, 1989.

Seow, C. L. *A Grammar for Biblical Hebrew* Rev. ed. Nashville: Abingdon, 1995.

Shimasaki, Katsuomi. *Focus Structure in Biblical Hebrew: A Study of Word Order and Information Structure*. Bethesda, MD: Capital Decisions, 2002.

Silva, Moises. *Biblical Words and Their Meaning: An Introduction to Lexical Semantics*. Grand Rapids: Zondervan, 1994.

Silzer, Peter James, and Thomas John Finley. *How Biblical Languages Work: A Student's Guide to Learning Hebrew and Greek*. Grand Rapids: Kregel Academic & Professional, 2004.

Siewierska, Anna. *Word Order Rules*. London: Routledge, 1988.

Simon, Ethelyn, Linda Motzkin, and Irene Resnikoff. *The First Hebrew Primer: The Adult Beginner's Path to Biblical Hebrew*. Oakland, CA: EKS Publishing, 2005.

Speiser, E. A. *Genesis*. Anchor Bible 1. Garden City: Doubleday, 1964.

Stubbs, Michael. *Discourse Analysis*. Chicago: University of Chicago, 1983.

Tonson, Paul. "Mercy Without Covenant: A Literary Analysis of Genesis 19." *JSOT* 95 (2001): 95–116

Tully, Eric J. *Hosea: A Handbook on the Hebrew Text*. Baylor Handbooks on the Hebrew Bible. Waco, TX: Baylor University Press, Forthcoming.

Walker-Jones, Arthur W. *Hebrew for Biblical Interpretation*. Atlanta: Society of Biblical Literature, 2003.

Ward, Gregory and Ellen Prince. "On the Topicalization of Indefinite

NP's." *J.Pragmat* 16 (1991): 161–77.

Waltke, Bruce and M. O'Connor. *An Introduction to Biblical Hebrew Syntax*. Winona Lake, IN: Eisenbrauns, 1990.

Webster, Brian L. *The Cambridge Introduction to Biblical Hebrew Paperback with CD-ROM*. Cambridge: Cambridge University, 2009.

Weingreen, J. *A Practical Grammar for Classical Hebrew*, 2nd ed. Oxford: Oxford University Press, 1959.

Wenham, Gordon J. *Genesis 26–50*. Word Biblical Commentary 2. Waco, TX: Word, 1994.

Wolde, Ellen van, ed. *Narrative Syntax and the Hebrew Bible: Papers of the Tilburg Conference 1996*. Leiden: Brill, 2002.

AUTHOR INDEX

SUBJECT INDEX

NOTES

www.ingramcontent.com/pod-product-compliance
Lightning Source LLC
Chambersburg PA
CBHW070039100426
42740CB00013B/2734